ARIZONA

PEARL Harbor
Dec 7, 1941

BY THE EDITORS OF CONSUMER GUIDE®

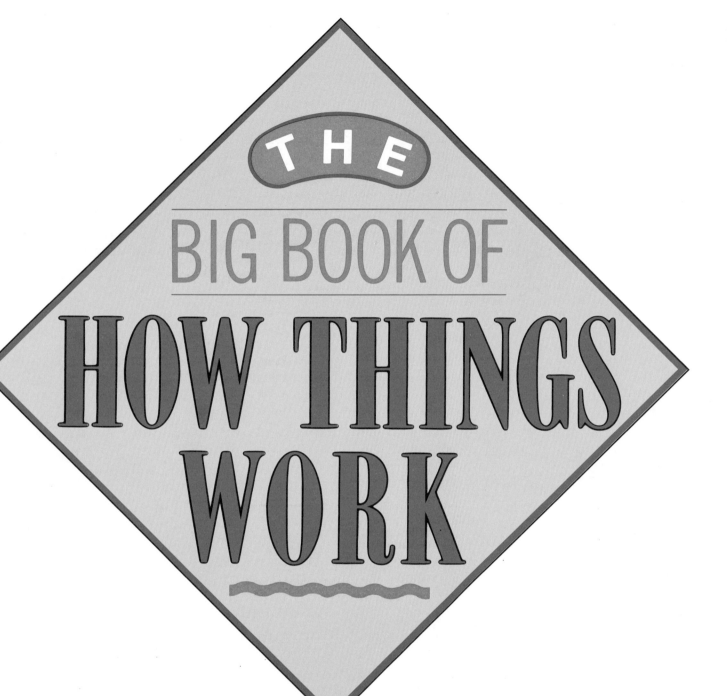

THE

BIG BOOK OF

HOW THINGS WORK

Contributing Writers:

Brent Butterworth
Lee Green

Consultant:

Joan Muratore

Illustrator:

Bill Whitney

PUBLICATIONS INTERNATIONAL, LTD.

CONTENTS

Contributors:

Brent Butterworth is a senior editor for *Video Magazine*. He has written for *Law Enforcement Technology* magazine and *Omni* magazine as well as technical articles on computers, flight simulators, construction materials, airplanes, and helicopters. He was a contributing author to CONSUMER GUIDE®'s *How Things Work*.

Lee Green is an engineer, free-lance writer, and computer programmer. He has taught music, physics, mathematics, and sailing and is currently involved in product testing. He was a contributing author to CONSUMER GUIDE®'s *How Things Work*.

Don Wulffson, who contributed the trivia items, teaches high school English, creative writing, and remedial reading. He is the author of *Incredible True Adventures*, *The Upside-Down Ship*, *The Invention of Ordinary Things*, *How Sports Came to Be*, and *Point-Blank* as well as more than 300 stories, poems, and plays for both children and adults.

Joan Muratore is a chemical engineer currently working for a consumer product-testing organization. Her projects have ranged from lipsticks to water filters.

Bill Whitney runs an illustration and production studio that specializes in creating editorial and commercial art using a variety of experimental mediums. He was the illustrator of CONSUMER GUIDE®'s *How Things Work*.

Special thanks to Paul Van Roy and Jane Otto, who assisted Bill Whitney in illustrating this book.

Louis Weber, C.E.O.
Publications International, Ltd.
7373 North Cicero Avenue
Lincolnwood, IL 60646

Permission is never granted for commercial purposes.

Manufactured in U.S.A.

h g f e d c b a

Library of Congress Catalog Card Number: 90-63493

ISBN: 1-56173-091-2

Hot-air balloon

How does a hot-air balloon fly?

Balloons rise because the gases inside them are lighter than the gases (air) outside them. Party balloons are filled with *helium* (HEE-lee-uhm) *gas*. Helium is lighter than air. It floats easily. Hot-air balloons are filled with air. The air in the balloon must be heated to make it lighter than the air around it. According to the law of *convection* (kuhn-VEK-shuhn), hot air rises.

Convection happens when a gas is heated. With balloons, the gas is air. As the gas heats up, its *molecules* (MAHL-i-kyoolz) move faster and faster. (A molecule is a particle that is so tiny, it is invisible to the eye. These particles, or pieces, join together to make up objects.)

As the molecules move faster, they move farther out. The gas *expands*. It takes up more space. This expanded gas is less *dense*, or lighter, than the gas around it. The heated gas rises. Cooler gas—air—moves in to take its place.

A **burner** heats the air inside the hot-air balloon. The burner runs on gas. The gas comes from a bottle. **Air heated by the burner** flows up into the balloon. The balloon begins to *inflate* (in-FLAYT). It fills up with air. After the ballon is filled, the passengers jump into the **basket**. (Some balloons have **sandbags** for extra weight. Extra weight keeps the basket from swinging around in the wind.)

Turning the heater's flame up or down controls the balloon. Turning up the flame heats the air inside the balloon. The balloon rises faster. Turning down the flame lets the air cool. The balloon drifts down.

A balloonist flies balloons across the sky. The balloonist lets the balloon rise until it reaches air that is blowing in the right direction. That air blows the balloon to the place the balloonist wishes to travel.

The hot-air balloon was invented by Jacques and Joseph Montgolfier. They were French brothers who ran a factory that made paper bags. They came up with the idea when they filled a paper bag with hot air and saw that it floated.

In 1783, they went for a test flight in their balloon. When they landed in a field, they scared the people around them. Because the people thought they were creatures from another planet, they cut the balloon into pieces.

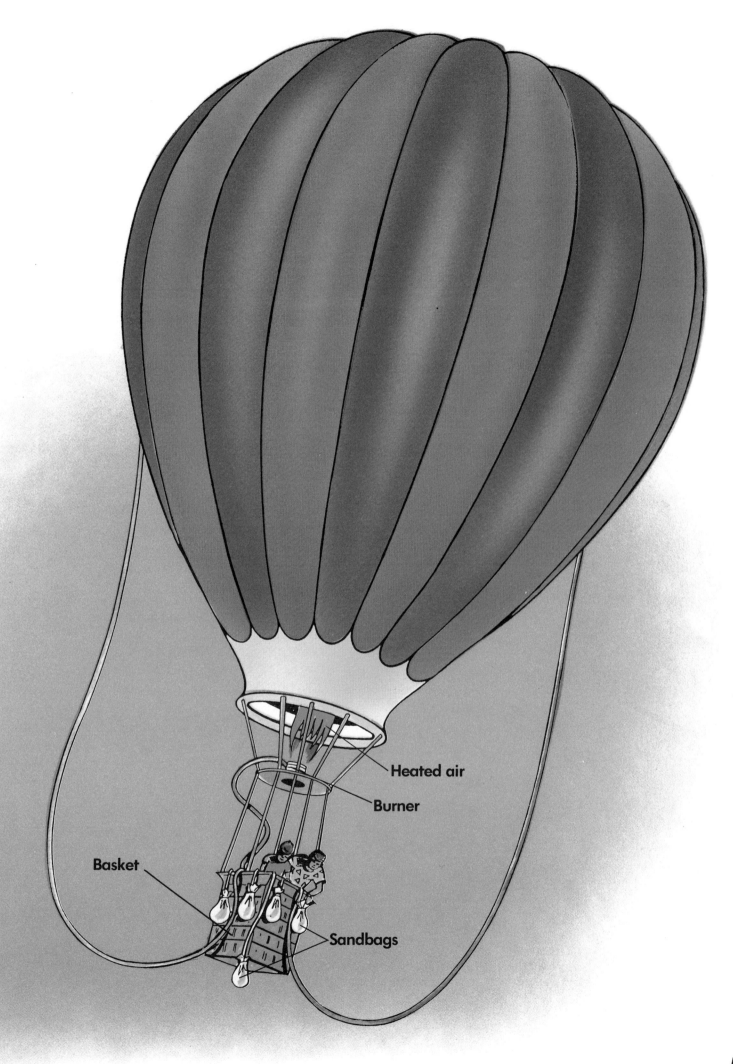

Heated air

Burner

Basket

Sandbags

5

Surfboard

How does a surfboard ride a wave?

A surfboard rides a wave because it is *buoyant* (BOY-uhnt)—it can float—and because it is pulled down the slope of water by *gravity*. (Gravity is the force that pulls us to the Earth. Without gravity, we would float.)

The trick in surfing is to slide across the wave. To surf, the surfer has to keep up with the wave. To keep up with the wave, the surfer has to match his or her speed to the wave's speed. Steering the board changes its speed. Steering downhill makes the board go faster. Steering uphill makes the board go slower.

To steer the board, the surfer leans back and lifts his or her weight off the front of the board. By shifting weight, the surfer can steer the board. To steer to the right, the surfer leans to the right and moves his or her weight backward. Because the **nose** of the board has little weight on it, it turns to the right. The **skeg** keeps the **tail** moving straight. (The skeg is a fish-like fin on the bottom of the board. Without a skeg, a surfboard would skid sideways down a wave.)

A coating on top of the board stops the surfer's feet from slipping. A **leash,** which goes around the ankle, keeps the board from drifting away when the surfer falls into the water.

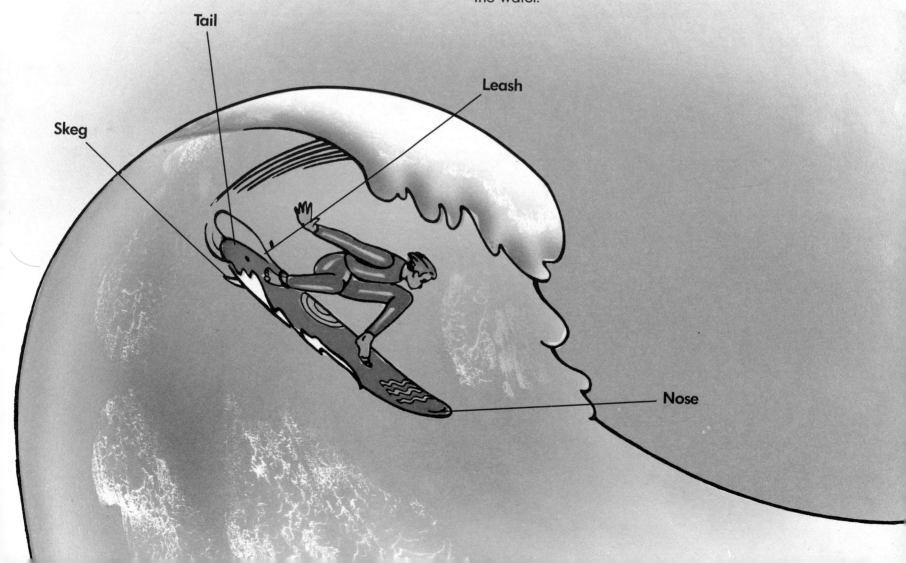

Tail

Skeg

Leash

Nose

Compass

Why does a compass needle always point north?

A compass needle always points north—when the compass is held flat. When you face the direction the needle is pointing, you are facing north. South is behind you, east is to your right, and west to your left.

Compasses work nearly everywhere on Earth. A compass is able to work *because* it is on Earth.

A **compass needle** is a magnet. A magnet is a metal that *attracts*, or pulls toward, some other metals. *Magnetism* (MAG-net-izm) is an invisible force that flows through these metals. Magnetism makes metals attract each other.

A magnet has two ends. The ends are the north pole and the south pole. The magnetic force flows out of the **north pole** and around to the south pole. It then flows back in to the south pole, through the magnet, and to the north pole. The area that the magnetic force flows through is the *magnetic field.*

Poles that are **opposite poles** attract each other. North poles attract south poles; south poles attract north poles. Poles that are **like poles** *repel*, or push away, each other.

The planet Earth is a magnet. Earth has a north pole and a south pole. The compass needle lines up with the Earth's lines of magnetic force. The magnetic force of the Earth makes the compass needle point north.

The compass needle spins on a thin post. Compasses have **markings.** They are N (north), S (south), E (east), and W (west).

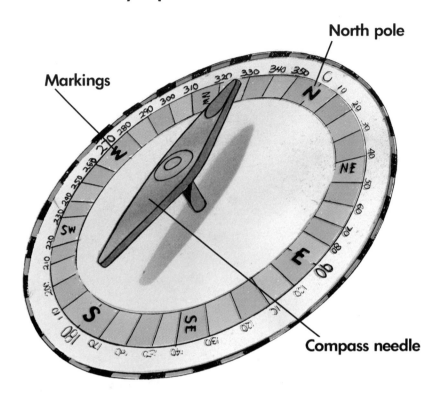

North pole

Markings

Compass needle

When the **opposite poles** of two magnets are placed near each other, the lines of force flow from one magnet to the other. The magnets attract each other.

When the **like poles** of two magnets are placed near each other, the lines of force flow back toward the other end of each magnet. The magnets repel each other.

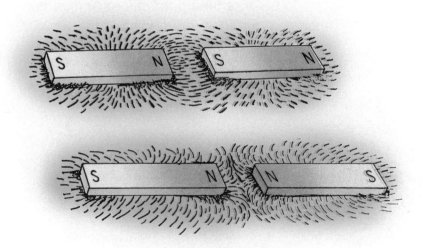

Teeter-totter

How can two people of different sizes ride a teeter-totter?

A playground teeter-totter, or see-saw, is a kind of *lever*. A lever is a tool. A lever moves heavy objects with little energy. A little person can balance or lift a big person on the teeter-totter because it is a lever.

The lever of the teeter-totter is the **board.** The **fulcrum** is what holds up the lever. The fulcrum of the teeter-totter holds up the center of the board.

The weight of the two riders presses down on each side of the fulcrum. The weight of the riders is the **force.** If the riders weigh the same—and sit the same distance away from the fulcrum—the force is equal. The board balances. This can be figured out with multiplication. First multiply the force on one side and its distance to the fulcrum. Then multiply the force on the other side and its distance to the fulcrum. If both sides are equal, the board balances.

If the riders do not weigh the same, the force is not equal. The board does not balance. The bigger person sinks to the ground.

To balance the board, the force must be evened out. There are two ways to even out the force. The fulcrum can be moved or the bigger person can move. To even out the force, the bigger person has to move closer to the fulcrum.

Let's take an example. One rider weighs 100 pounds and another rider weighs 50 pounds. The 100-pound rider must sit twice as close to the fulcrum as the 50-pound rider sits. (This is because 100 pounds is twice as heavy as 50 pounds.)

By keeping the teeter-totter balanced between the two riders, they will both be able to push off the ground in turn. They will "teeter" on the fulcrum. When they are high in the air, they "see." When they are down, they "saw!"

Force

Board

Fulcrum

9

Aquarium

Why don't the fish in an aquarium ever run out of air to breathe?

1. Fish, like people and animals, breathe oxygen. They take it from the water. Lakes and oceans have plenty of water—and oxygen—to go around. In an aquarium, new oxygen must replace the used oxygen. Aquariums put oxygen back into the water with an **air pump.** A common air pump is a belt-driven piston pump.

2. In this kind of pump, an **electric motor** makes the belt move.

3. The **belt** loops around a pulley. (A pulley is a wheel with a groove. The belt rides in the groove.)

4. As the belt turns the **pulley,** the pulley pushes and pulls the piston. (A piston is a short rod that slides back and forth in a cylinder.)

5. When the **piston** pulls back, it sucks air through an intake valve. (A valve is a small tube through which things flow.) When the piston pushes forward, the air is forced through tubing.

6. The cylinder's **intake valve** is a one-way valve. It lets air in, but it doesn't let it out. Another one-way valve at the end of the air hose lets the air out, but will not let water in.

7. The **tubing** leads to the aquarium's filter. Air coming in pushes water from the aquarium through the filter. The filter cleans the water. After the air does its work inside the filter, it flows out of the filter. The air bubbles float to the top of the tank. The water *absorbs* some of the oxygen from these air bubbles like a sponge absorbs water. The fish have oxygen to breathe.

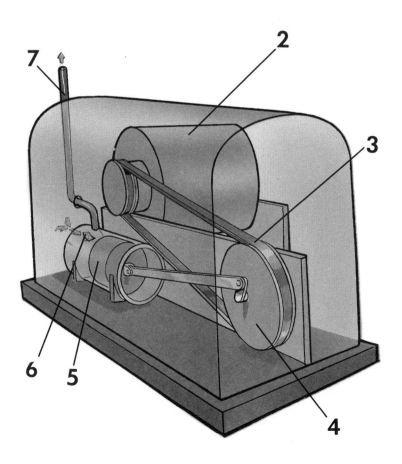

Soap bubbles

How can bubbles be made from soap?

Bubbles can be made from soap because, like people, water has a "skin." (Without this skin, water could not make drops. The water's skin holds the water in.)

The water's skin is made of *molecules* (MAHL-i-kyoolz). A molecule is a particle that is so tiny, it is invisible to the eye. These particles, or pieces, stick together to form the skin. The skin is caused by surface tension. A drop of water hangs on the edge of a faucet because of surface tension. The molecules of the water stick together to keep the drop from breaking. A small insect can walk across water because of surface tension. The surface tension is strong enough to carry the insect's weight. In a bubble, the skin acts like a balloon filled with air.

You can't blow bubbles with plain water. The surface tension of water is strong—it will not stretch far. Soap or detergent makes the surface tension less strong. It lets the skin stretch. Too little soap doesn't let the skin stretch enough. Too much soap lets the skin stretch too much. Just the right amount of soap in water will let you make bubbles.

A bubble wand is a favorite way to make bubbles. Dipping the wand into the soapy liquid coats the loop with soap. Blowing air into the circle or waving the wand fills the film of soap with air. The pocket of air grows until the end of the stretchy film shuts. A bubble is born!

The soap film in the loop of a bubble wand changes shape as the shape of the wand changes. Bubbles are round most of the time. A round shape stretches the skin evenly in all directions.

Pinball machine

What makes the balls bounce and move around in a pinball machine?

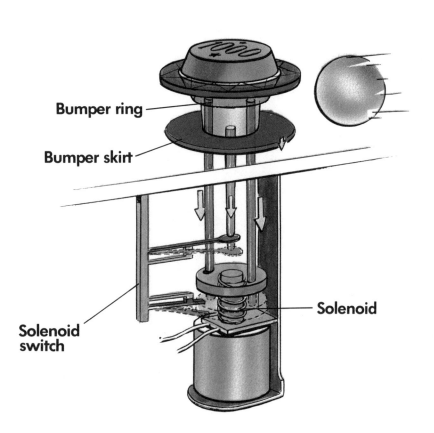

Bumper ring

Bumper skirt

Solenoid switch

Solenoid

1. The ball rolls toward the **bumper.**

2. The ball pushes down on the **bumper skirt**, sending electricity to the solenoid.

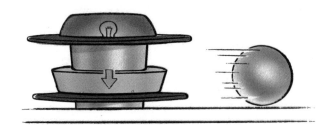

3. The solenoid pulls the **bumper ring** down, knocking the pinball away.

Pinball machines use *gravity* to keep the pinball rolling. (Gravity is the force that pulls us to the Earth. Without gravity, we would float.) Because the table—the top of the pinball machine—is slanted, gravity pulls the ball toward the pit at the bottom of the table. To keep the ball in play, you must keep it away from the pit.

Drop a coin into the slot and a ball loads up in front of the shooter. Pull back on the shooter and let go. A spring shoots the steel

ball up to the top of the table. The ball rolls and bumps down the table. As the ball gets near the bottom, shoot it back up with the flippers. Each side of the table has a button that works a flipper. Some machines have two sets of flippers. One set is near the middle. The other set is near the bottom.

Pushing the flipper buttons on the side of the machine sends electricity to the flipper. The flipper is connected to a **solenoid** (SO-luh-noyd). A solenoid is a *coil*, or loop,

In 1939, the city of Atlanta, Georgia, made playing pinball machines a crime. The punishment was a $20 fine and a month in jail.

of wires with a metal rod inside. The rod is *magnetic*—it acts like a magnet. When electricity flows through the coil, it makes a *magnetic field*. The magnetic field pulls on the rod, and the rod moves the flipper. The flipper hits the ball back up the table. As the ball comes back down, it hits a bumper.

Each bumper uses its own solenoid to kick the ball around. Behind the bumper is a **solenoid switch.** The pinball, bouncing around, hits the **bumper skirt.** As the

bumper skirt goes down, it pushes on the switch. Flipping the switch sends electricity to the bumper solenoid. The solenoid switch sends a burst of electricity to a computer inside the pinball machine. The computer then adds the number of points and displays them on the back panel of the machine. The solenoid also pulls the **bumper ring** down. As the bumper ring goes down, it knocks away the pinball.

Kaleidoscope

How does a kaleidoscope make so many different patterns?

Although the patterns seem endless and the designs look complex, the kaleidoscope (kuh-LYD-uh-skop) is a simple invention.

At one end of the cardboard tube is a **peephole.** At the other end are **two sheets of glass.** The inside sheet is made of clear glass. The outside sheet is made of glass that has been ground up. **Bits of colored glass, beads,** or **metal chips** are sandwiched between the sheets.

A **pair of long, flat mirrors** runs along the tube. The mirrors face each other. They make a V shape with an angle of 60°. As

light shines through the plates of glass, the mirrors reflect the image. The image is of the colored bits. The reflections are *repeated.* They are shown again and again. Because of repeated reflections, the mirrors show **five images.** The sixth image you see is of the real colored glass bits, beads, or metal chips. Peeping through the hole, you see the same colored design six times.

When you turn the tube, the colored pieces move, forming a brand-new pattern.

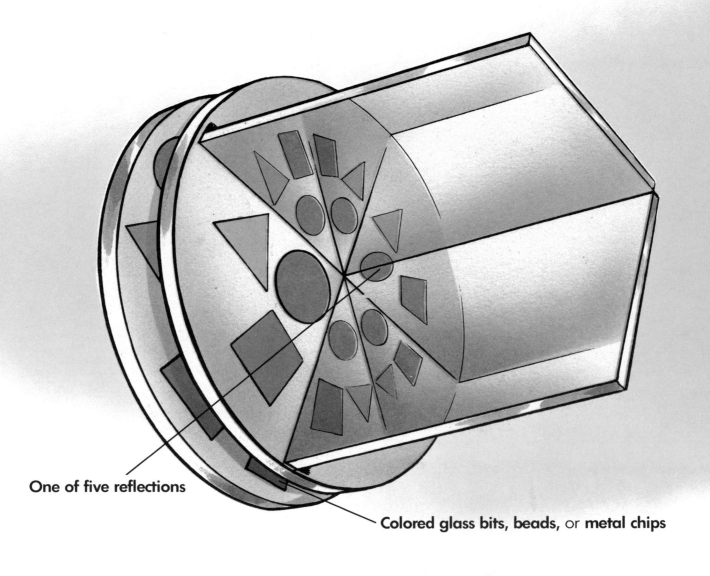

One of five reflections

Colored glass bits, beads, or **metal chips**

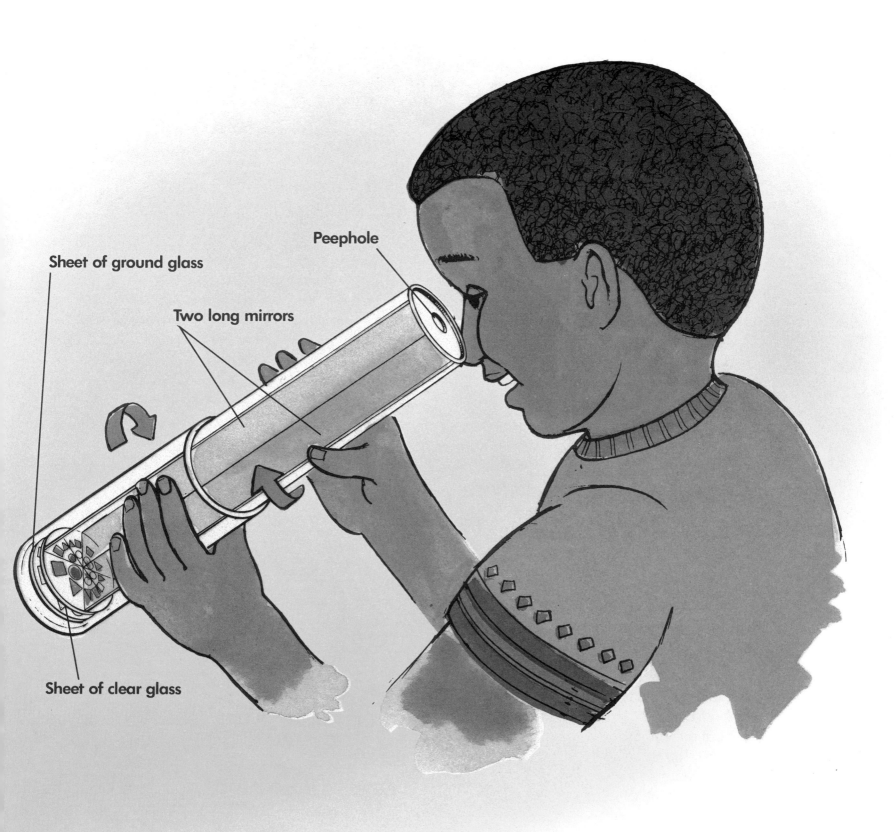

Sheet of ground glass

Peephole

Two long mirrors

Sheet of clear glass

Sailboat

How does wind drive a sailboat across the water?

The sail of a sailboat uses the blowing wind to move the sailboat along.

When sailing with the wind, the sail catches the wind. As the wind blows into the sail, it pushes the boat.

When sailing into the wind, air strikes the sail and divides. The sail curves out. Some of the air goes on one side of the sail, some of it goes on the other side. The air flowing on the outside of the curved sail has farther to travel in the same time than the air flowing on the inside of the curved sail.

Since it has farther to go in the same time, the air on the outside of the curve must go faster than the air on the inside of the curve. As the air speed gets faster, its pressure gets lower. The air on the outside of the curve has faster speed and lower pressure. The air on the inside of the curve has slower speed and higher pressure.

The difference in the two pressures causes *lift*. The boat is pulled forward by the lift created as the wind passes over its sails. The lift drives the boat.

A sailboat with two sails can get even more drive from the wind. The sail in front of the boat is the **jib,** and the sail in back is the **mainsail.** The jib does two things. It uses the wind to create lift. It also directs air between itself and the outside of the curve of the mainsail. Squeezing air—as when it goes between the jib and the mainsail—makes the air go faster. As the air between the jib and mainsail goes faster, the drive gets stronger.

A sailboat can sail in a direction in which the wind is not blowing by *tacking*. The sailboat follows a course that is at a slight angle to the wind. By zigzagging at angles into the wind, a boat can reach its target.

The sailboat has built-in controls. The **keel** is a heavy, fish-like fin on the bottom of the boat. It keeps the boat from tipping over in rough weather and high waves. The **rudder** steers the boat. It keeps the boat on course.

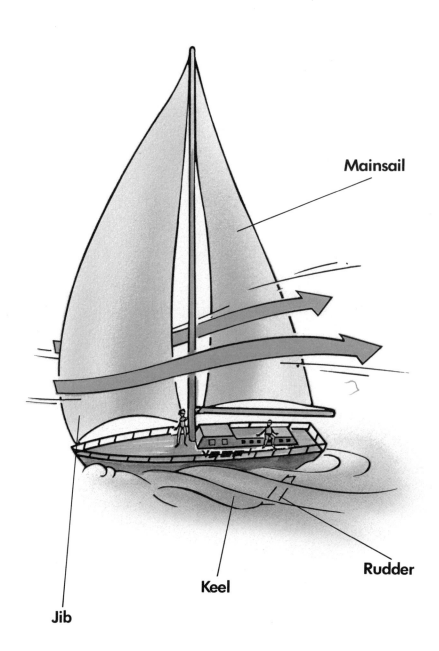

Mainsail

Rudder

Keel

Jib

Yo-yo

What makes a yo-yo go up and down?

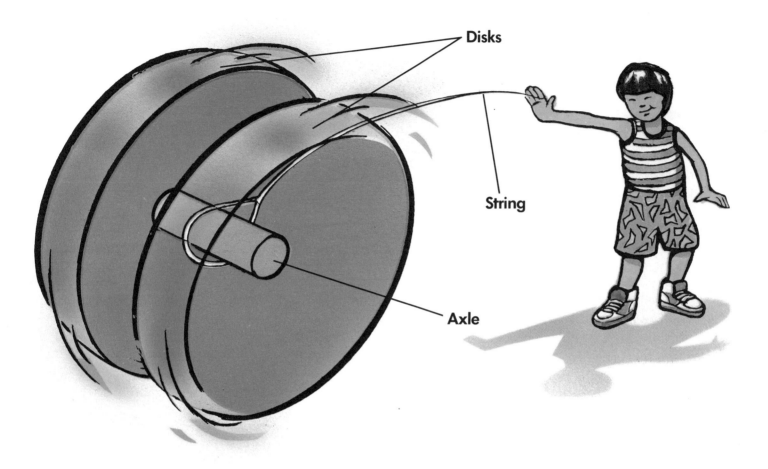

Disks

String

Axle

Throwing the yo-yo down—with your finger looped through one end of the **string**—starts the yo-yo spinning. The spinning makes the yo-yo act like a *gyroscope* (JY-ro-skop). A gyroscope spins in the same direction until *gravity* slows it down. (Gravity is the force that pulls to the Earth. Without gravity, we would float.) The *gyrating* (JY-rayt-ing) action keeps the yo-yo from twisting and unwinding the string.

The string is tied around the **axle.** The axle is the short, smooth rod that connects the two **disks** of the yo-yo. If the string is

wound tightly around the axle, the yo-yo comes back up as it reaches the end of the string. *Friction* (FRIK-shuhn) between the string and the axle makes the yo-yo return. Friction keeps the axle from slipping away from the string. The yo-yo spins back up the string.

If the string is not wound tightly around the axle, the yo-yo keeps on spinning at the end of the string. There is not enough friction between the string and the axle. The axle slips around inside the loop of string. Tugging on the string creates enough friction to make the yo-yo climb back up the string.

Subway train

What makes a subway train run?

Subway trains run on electricity.

A subway track has two **main rails** on which the train rolls. A third rail is the **electric rail.** The third rail can be between the main tracks or off to one side. It carries 500 to 700 volts of electricity—much more powerful than the electricity running through your home.

Electricity travels through a *circuit,* or loop. The circuit in a subway train goes from the tracks to the cars and back again.

To get from the track to the train, electricity flows through a **conducting shoe.** (A conducting shoe is a piece of metal that touches the third rail.) From the conducting shoe, electricity flows to the train's motors, lights, and doors. Electricity also runs the train's heating and air-conditioning systems.

The train's motors sit inside its **trucks.** The trucks hold the train's **axles.** (An axle is a rod that has a wheel on each end.) The train's wheels are made of steel. The wheels *conduct,* or move, electricity out of the train and back to the main tracks. The circuit is complete.

The train's driver controls the train with a **lever.** Pushing the lever forward sends the train forward. Letting the lever move back into place slows and stops the train.

Subway cars can be added to the train if the train has to carry a lot of people. Subway cars can be subtracted from the train if there are only a few people to carry. In the morning, a dozen cars may be hooked together by a **hitch.** Late at night, a car may run alone.

Hitch

There are 67 underground railway systems in use in the world today. The first was built in London, England, in 1863. The first in the United States opened in Boston, Massachusetts, in 1898. The New York City subway opened in 1904. It has more than 200 miles of tracks. It is the world's largest underground railway system.

Air vent to street level

Lever

Truck

Axle

Conducting shoe

Main rails

Electric rail

19

Eyeglasses

How do eyeglasses help people see better?

For a person to see an image clearly, the image must be *focused,* or shown clearly, inside the eye. The image should focus on the eye's **retina** (RET-i-nuh). The retina is like a movie screen on the back wall of the eyeball. Light enters the eye through the **cornea** (KOR-nee-uh). Behind the cornea is the clear eye **lens** that focuses light on the retina. The iris gives eyes their color. The pupil is the black center opening of the iris.

Some people are *farsighted.* What they see far away looks clear. What they see close up looks blurry. Other people are *nearsighted.* What they see close up looks clear. What they see far away looks blurry. Eyeglass lenses of different shapes clear up the blurry images.

Convex lenses make farsighted people see up close. Convex lenses curve out. Concave lenses make nearsighted people see far away. Concave lenses curve in.

The first eyeglasses were held in front of the eyes by a handle. Other eyeglasses were tied to the head by a ribbon. Still other glasses clipped onto the nose like a clothespin.

Retina   **Lens**   **Cornea**   **Convex lens**

Uncorrected farsightedness   **Corrected farsightedness**

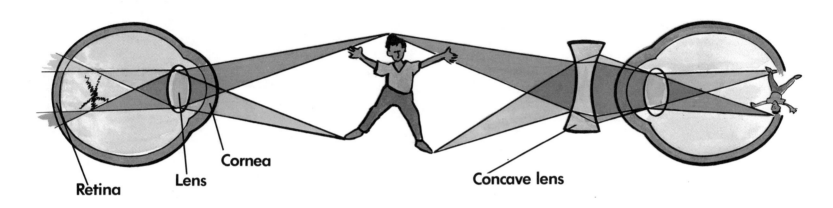

Retina   **Lens**   **Cornea**   **Concave lens**

Uncorrected nearsightedness   **Corrected nearsightedness**

The shape of a farsighted eye is shorter than the shape of a normal eye. When it looks at a close-up object, it forms an image. This image focuses behind, not on, the retina. The brain sees a fuzzy picture. A faraway object focuses on the retina. The brain sees a clear picture. A lens that makes a close-up image seem farther away will help the eye see better.

A **convex lens** bends light rays in. The rays seem to come from farther away. The light can then be focused on the retina as in a normal eye. The farsighted eye then clearly sees things near and far.

The shape of a nearsighted eye is longer than the shape of a normal eye. When it looks at a faraway object, it forms an image. This image focuses in front of, not on, the retina. Again, the brain sees a fuzzy picture. A close-up image focuses on the retina. The brain sees a clear picture. A lens that makes a faraway image seem closer will help the eye see better.

A **concave lens** bends light rays out. The rays seem to come from close up. The light can then be focused on the retina as in a normal eye. The nearsighted eye then clearly sees things far and near.

Compact disc player

How does a compact disc player play music differently from a record player?

The biggest difference between a compact disc and a record is one you can't see. Records and compact discs (called CDs) do not record sound in the same way.

On a record, grooves *represent*, or stand for, sound. (A groove is a thin, deep path. The groove on a record looks like a long line that winds around and around.) During recording, the grooves are cut into the record. During playback, the record player's needle reads the grooves and changes them back into sound.

On a CD, tiny dents and spaces make a pattern that represents sound. The dents and spaces are on the bottom side of the CD. During recording, the dents are burned into the CD. During playback, a laser inside the compact disc player points at the bottom of the disc. (A laser is a narrow beam of light.) As the CD turns, the laser light passes over the dents and spaces. The laser acts as if the CD were a mirror. It *reflects*, or sends back, the bursts of light into the player. The player changes the bursts of light into signals. The CD player then reads the signals. The speakers change the signals back into sound.

Telescope

How does a telescope make faraway objects look closer?

A simple kind of telescope is made of two tubes and three lenses. One of the **tubes** fits inside the other. A large glass lens is at one end of the tubes. It is the **objective.** The objective points at the object. A lens that *magnifies,* or makes things look bigger, is held to the eye. It is the **eyepiece.** An eyepiece can be made up of one lens or many lenses. A telescope lens has great magnifying power.

All objects give off light. Light travels in **light waves.** Light waves travel from the **object** to the telescope. The light waves pass through the objective and into the tube of the telescope. The image looks upside down. Halfway down the tube is a **middle lens.** The middle lens bends the light waves to turn the image right-side up. The image reaches the eyepiece right-side up.

The eyepiece magnifies the faraway image. One of the tubes slides in and out of the other so the telescope can be *focused.* (Focusing means to make something look clear.) Sliding the tube changes the distance between the objective and the eyepiece. When this distance is just right, the image becomes focused. The image of the object seen through the telescope is clear.

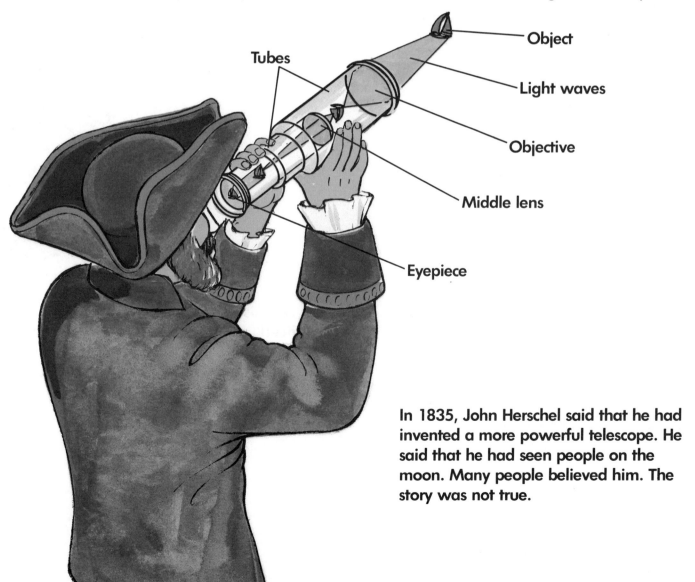

Tubes

Object

Light waves

Objective

Middle lens

Eyepiece

In 1835, John Herschel said that he had invented a more powerful telescope. He said that he had seen people on the moon. Many people believed him. The story was not true.

Electronic keyboard

How does an electronic keyboard make so many sounds?

Music is a special form of sound. Sound is made up of *air vibrations* (vy-BRAY-shuhnz). An air vibration is the back-and-forth movement of air. Air vibrations can be changed into electrical signals by a microphone. The changing signals are changed back into sound by a loudspeaker.

An electronic keyboard can make the electrical signals itself, without the original sound or a microphone.

All notes have different frequencies (FREE-kwuhn-seez), sizes, and shapes. (Frequencies are speeds.) Notes can be made up of one frequency or many different ones. This is why a trumpet sounds different from a guitar—even when they play the same note. An electronic keyboard can sound like different instruments because it can make electrical signals that have the same note speed, size, and shape of many instruments.

The electrical signals go from the keyboard to the speakers. What comes out of the speaker sounds the same as what an instrument would sound like.

Keyboards can even make sounds that an instrument can't make. A keyboard records real sounds with a microphone. The sound may be a voice, a knock at the door, or a bird's chirp. The keyboard's memory "remembers" the size and shape of a sound. It can change the size and shape of the sound. The keyboard can record a bird chirping, and play back what sounds like a bird singing "Happy Birthday!"

Scientists have learned that outer space is filled with many sounds. During a space mission, radio waves from space were sent back to Earth. The sounds of outer space were found to be birdlike chirps, booming sounds, and whistles.

Clocks and watches

How do clocks and watches keep time?

All clocks and watches have three basic parts. One part *stores*, or holds, energy. Another part *releases*, or gives off, the energy. The energy is released as a group of *pulses*. (A pulse is a beat.) The third part counts the pulses. For a clock or watch to keep time, the pulses must be made at an even rate.

A **pendulum** (PEND-yoo-luhm) keeps the rate even in a clock. A pendulum is made up of a rod and a weight at the end of the rod. It is attached to the clock. It swings back and forth. A push starts the pendulum swinging. It takes the pendulum exactly the same time to swing back as it did to swing forth. A long pendulum takes a longer time to complete a swing; a short one takes a shorter time.

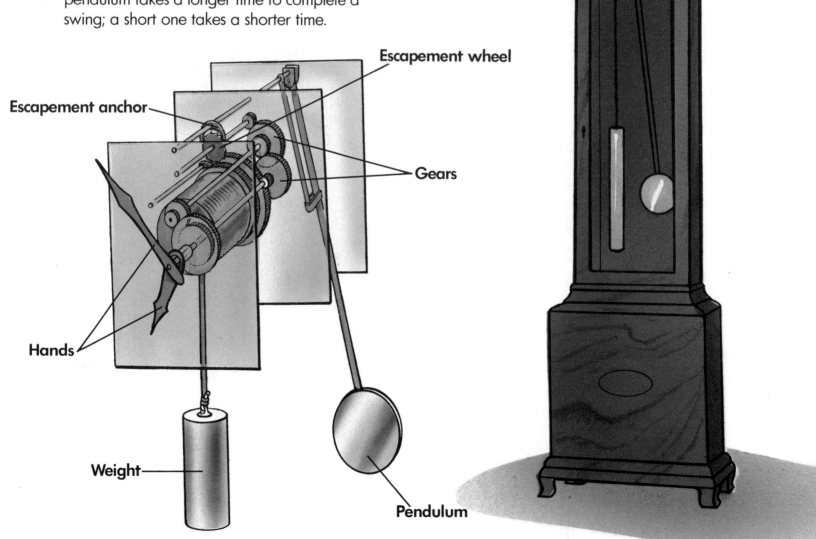

Escapement wheel

Escapement anchor

Gears

Hands

Weight

Pendulum

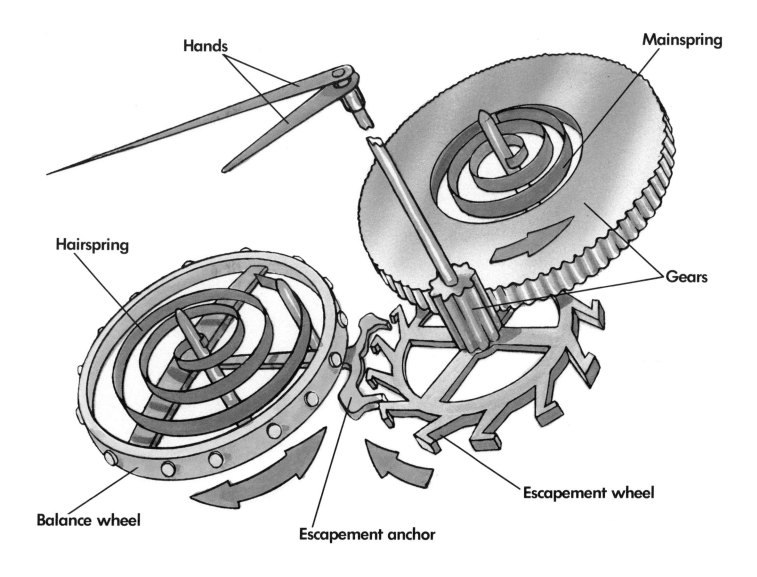

Hands

Mainspring

Hairspring

Gears

Balance wheel

Escapement wheel

Escapement anchor

The energy to run the clock is stored by winding a gear. (A gear is a wheel with pointy teeth.) Winding the gear raises a heavy **weight.** The weight gear is connected to other gears that turn the **hands** of the clock.

The pendulum is attached to an *escapement*. The escapement is made up of a wheel and an anchor. The **escapement wheel** has teeth on it. It is a gear. The **escapement anchor** has two ends. Each end has one point on it. The escapement controls the gear that turns the other **gears.**

When the pendulum swings one way, one end of the escapement anchor catches a tooth on the escapement wheel. The gears stop turning for a moment. When the pendulum swings back the other way, the anchor lets go of the tooth it was holding. It catches

another tooth on the wheel with its other end. The gears turn just a little.

The weight drops a tiny bit with each swing of the pendulum. Each time the weight drops, it sends a small push through the gears and escapement. The push keeps the pendulum swinging. The clock will run until the weight has dropped as far as it can go. Winding the clock raises the weight.

A watch works like a clock. A **balance wheel** acts like the pendulum. A **mainspring** acts like the weight. The mainspring stores energy when it is wound up. The balance wheel is attached to a **hairspring.** The hairspring is the watch's escapement. The escapement pulls the balance wheel back and forth, back and forth. This is the same push that a pendulum is given.

Neon light

Why does a neon light glow?

A neon light uses electricity and gas to glow. The **glass tubing** is filled with **neon gas.** The electricity flows through the gas.

A **high-voltage transformer** changes the electricity to high-voltage electricity. Its high voltage makes the electricity able to excite the gas. Exciting the gas lets the electricity flow from one end of the tube to the other. As the high-voltage electricity runs through the gas, it makes the neon in the tube glow.

Different gases glow different colors. Neon gas glows red. Powders added to the tubing and shaded tubing can create many colors.

To make a neon sign, glass tubing is bent into a shape. Letters, words, and pictures can be made.

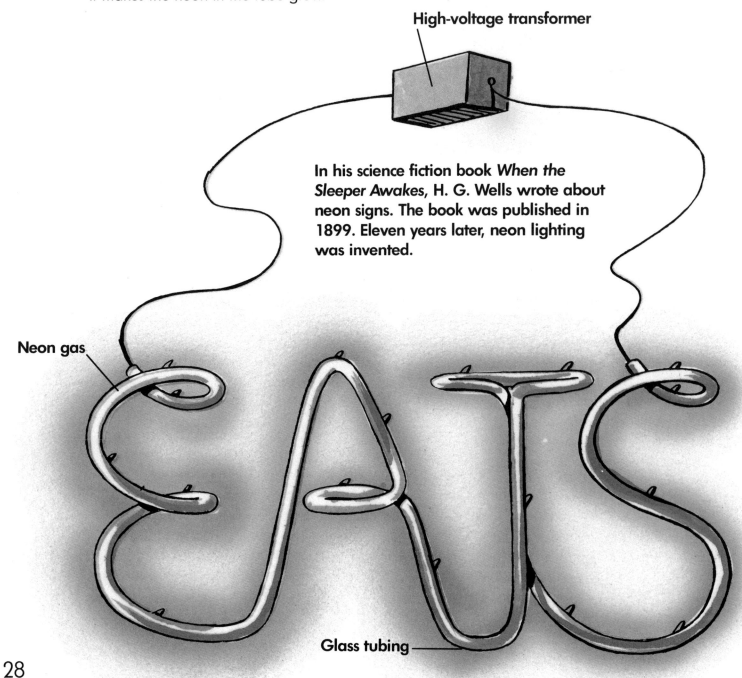

High-voltage transformer

In his science fiction book *When the Sleeper Awakes*, H. G. Wells wrote about neon signs. The book was published in 1899. Eleven years later, neon lighting was invented.

Neon gas

Glass tubing

Scooter

What makes a scooter go?

Handlebars

Caliper brakes

Spinning wheels

Even the best scooters made today do not use chains, gears, or pedals to make them go. Their power and speed is "all in the foot."

As your foot pushes off the ground, the scooter moves forward. A few good pushes will send the scooter off at a good speed. Once the scooter is rolling, a push now and then will keep up the speed. Going downhill is a free ride—*gravity* pulls the scooter down. (Gravity is the force that pulls us to the Earth. Without gravity, we would float.)

The scooter's **spinning wheels** act like *gyroscopes* (JY-ro-skops). A gyroscope spins in the same direction until gravity slows it down. The wheels of the scooter will stand up straight as long as they are spinning fast enough. This is gyroscopic (jy-ro-SKAHP-ik) force.

To steer to the right, the rider turns the **handlebars** to the right. To steer left, the rider turns the handlebars left.

There are two ways to stop. The rider can put one foot down on the ground. Or the rider can use the scooter's **caliper brakes** (if the scooter has them). Squeezing the brake handles make rubber brake shoes press against the rim of the front wheel. As the rubber brake shoes squeeze the rim, *friction* (FRIK-shuhn) is created. Friction makes the scooter slow down. When the scooter begins to wobble, the rider can put a foot down to come to a safe stop.

Photocopier

How does a photocopying machine make copies?

1. The page to be copied is placed face down on the **glass window.**

2. **Bright lights** sweep across the image on the page.

3. **Mirrors** reflect the light from the image onto an aluminum drum.

4. The **drum** is covered with a *photoconductor*. (A photoconductor conducts electricity—it helps electricity flow—when light shines on it.)

5. The drum turns against a **corona.** A corona gives the drum a **positive electric charge.** (The positive charges are shown here by the "+" signs.)

6. Wherever the **reflected image** is dark, the drum has a positive charge. Wherever the reflected image is light, the charge disappears.

7. The **toner** is given a negative charge. (The negative charges are shown here as tiny circles.) The toner is a black chemical powder. Just as with a magnet, the negative charge is *attracted* to the positive charge. The negative charge goes toward the positive charge. The toner is attracted to parts of the drum that represent, or stand for, the dark parts of the image being copied.

8. To get the toner to leave the drum and stick to the paper, the paper is given a positive charge. Another **corona** between the paper and drum gives the paper the charge. The positive charge given to the paper is stronger than the positive charge given to the drum. The toner powder is attracted off the drum and onto the paper.

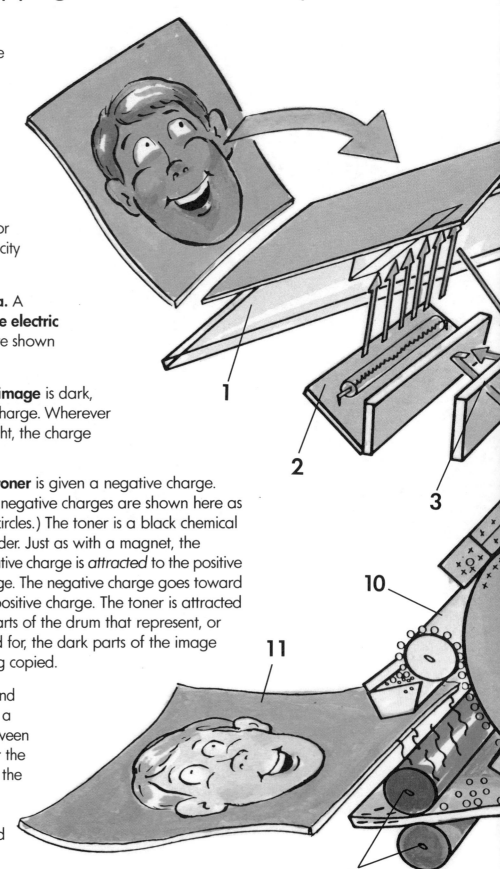

Chester Carlson invented the photocopier in 1938. Not one company wanted to build his machine. Ten years later, a small company called the Haloid Company said they would build it. Today, the Haloid Company is the giant Xerox Corporation.

9. The paper passes though **two hot rollers**. The heat melts the toner powder. The rollers turn the black powder image into an image that can't be erased.

10. The drum must roll to a **cleaning area** after every copy the machine makes. Old toner is cleaned off; new toner can be attached for another copy. This happens in less than a second.

11. The **copy** slides out of the machine. It may be hard to tell it from the original!

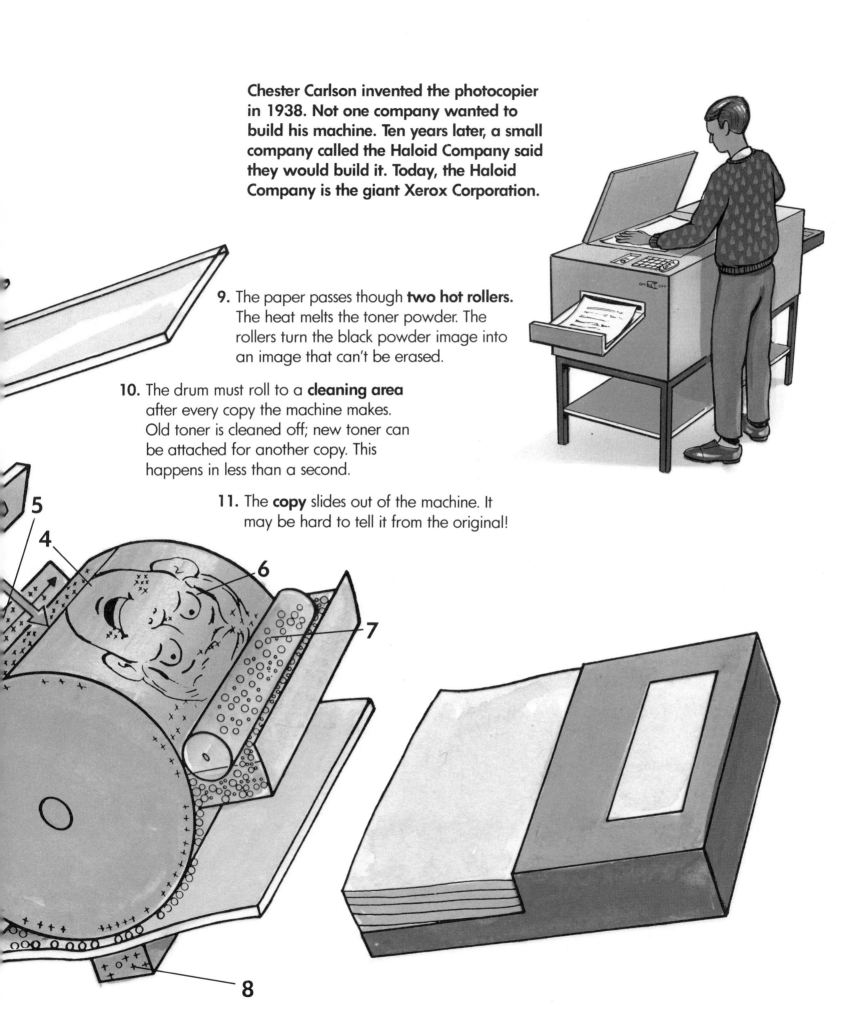

Roller coaster

Where does a roller coaster get the energy to ride around and around?

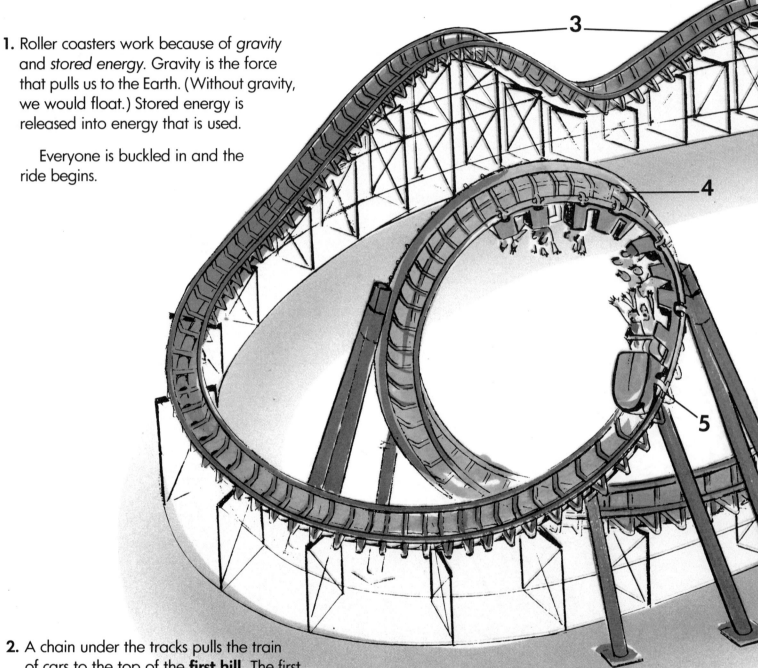

1. Roller coasters work because of *gravity* and *stored energy*. Gravity is the force that pulls us to the Earth. (Without gravity, we would float.) Stored energy is released into energy that is used.

Everyone is buckled in and the ride begins.

2. A chain under the tracks pulls the train of cars to the top of the **first hill.** The first hill is the highest of the ride. All of a roller coaster's energy comes from being pulled up the first hill. The roller coaster stores energy as it is being pulled up the first hill. Gravity pulls the cars down the hill. The power for the rest of the ride comes from the pull of gravity and stored energy—not from motors and chains.

3. The **hills** of a roller coaster cannot be higher than the first one. Not enough energy is stored in the roller coaster to climb that high again. Each hill the cars climb uses more energy than can be stored in the next run down the hill.

2

1

5. The cars of a loop roller coaster have **wheels** that touch the top, side, and bottom of the track. These extra wheels make sure the cars stay on the track. Side wheels keep the car from slipping sideways. Bottom wheels hold an upside-down car onto the track. Friction is created as the wheels rub against the tracks. Friction slows the cars down. The operator can then stop the cars with the brakes.

4. Going around a **loop** makes a roller coaster act like a *gyroscope* (JY-ro-skop). A gyroscope spins in the same direction until gravity and *friction* (FRIK-shuhn) slow it down. (Friction is created when two things rub against each other.) The roller coaster keeps moving in the same direction and at the same speed until gravity and friction stop it.

The cars of a roller coaster would keep moving outward in a loop if there were not any tracks. The tracks make the cars go around in a circle. *Gyroscopic* (jy-ro-SKAHP-ik) *force* plus the speed of the traveling car presses you into your seat. You don't fall out when the roller coaster makes a loop.

5

33

Rocket engine

What makes a rocket blast off?

A basic rocket engine is filled with fuel. When the fuel is lit, it burns. The rocket moves because every action has an equal and opposite reaction. The *action* is the hot gases exploding out of the rocket. The hot gases come out with great force. This action causes a *reaction*. The reaction is the forward motion (blasting off) of the rocket. The reaction has the equal force in the opposite direction. Because the gases shoot down, the rocket shoots up.

There are two types of rockets: solid-fuel rockets and liquid-fuel rockets. Fireworks on the Fourth of July are launched into the sky by solid-fuel rockets. Solid-fuel rockets have tubes packed with a fuel. The fuel is in solid form.

The *Saturn V* used on the moon missions is a liquid-fuel rocket. Liquid-fuel rockets have separate tanks. One **tank** carries the liquid **fuel**—usually hydrogen. Another **tank** carries liquid **oxygen**. Fuel cannot burn without oxygen. Space rockets burn so much fuel so fast, they need more oxygen than the air around them can give. Also, there is no oxygen in outer space. The rockets must carry their own oxygen.

The fuel and oxygen are combined in the **combustion chamber**. **Pumps** make the fuel and oxygen flow to the chamber. **Valves** start and stop the flow of the fuel and the oxygen. Once in the combustion chamber, the fuel and oxygen burn and explode. The **burning gases** shoot out through the nozzle.

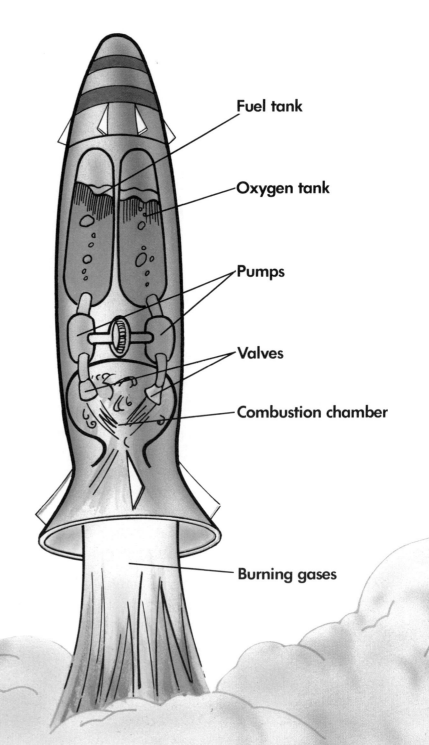

Fuel tank

Oxygen tank

Pumps

Valves

Combustion chamber

Burning gases

Popcorn poppers

What makes corn pop?

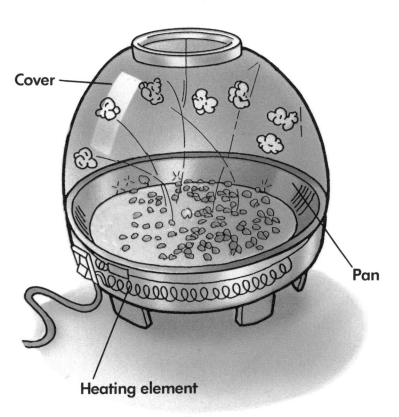

Cover

Pan

Heating element

Hot-oil popper

Inside a dried popcorn kernel is starch and a little water. When the popcorn kernel is heated, the starch inside the kernel *expands*. The starch takes up more room. The temperature inside the hull (the outer covering of the kernel) gets hotter and hotter. The pressure increases as the temperature gets hotter until the hull breaks open. The bit of water flashes into steam. The steam creates a puff of starch and air. It's popcorn!

Where is most of the popcorn in the United States eaten? Ninety percent of all popcorn is eaten at home—not at the movies.

A **hot-oil popper** is one way to pop corn. Electricity flows through the **heating element**. As electricity flows, the heating element heats the **pan**. The pan holds oil and kernels. The pan's **cover** keeps the kernels from escaping as they pop. The oil coats the popcorn and helps to heat each kernel evenly. It also keeps the popped corn from burning on the bottom of the pan.

A **hot-air popper** is another way to pop corn. Electricity runs a **motor**. The motor heats the **heating element**. Very hot air, not oil, heats the kernels evenly. A **fan** blows the hot air up through a **screen** and into the **popping chamber**. As the kernels pop, they become large, fluffy, and light. The hot air blows the popped corn through the **chute**.

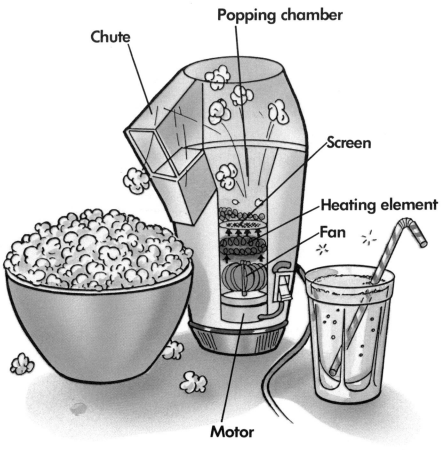

Chute

Popping chamber

Screen

Heating element

Fan

Motor

Hot-air popper

35

Electricity
How does electricity get into our homes?

1. The electricity in your home comes from a power plant. Some power plants get their power from water. The water flow of a river can be controlled by a **dam**. A dam has walls. Water flows through the walls.

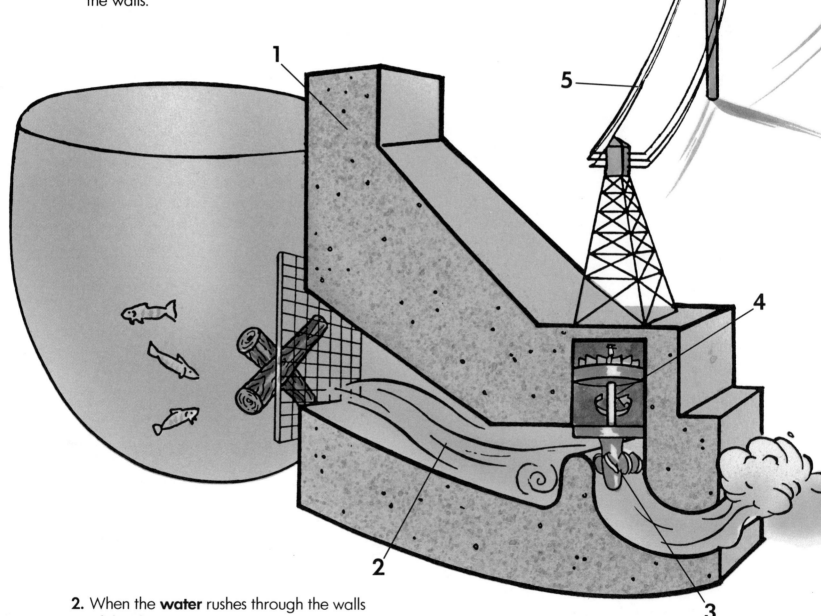

2. When the **water** rushes through the walls of the dam, it creates pressure.

3. Water pressure turns the **blades** of the shaft of the **generator**. The shaft powers the generator as it spins.

4. As the **shaft** turns, electricity flows through *coils* of wire. (A coil is a loop.) Flowing through the wire makes the electricity stronger. There are many generators in a power plant. Together, their power is great.

5. Electricity flows out of the generator and through **power lines**. The lines lead to a transformer near your house.

6. The **transformer** brings the power down to a level that is safe for use in your home. Transformers can be seen atop power-line poles. The power lines are strung between the poles.

7. Electricity travels through another line to a **meter** on your house. The meter marks how much electricity you have used and how much electricity you must pay for. Electricity comes into the house through the meter.

Electricity flows through wiring that is between the walls of your house. The wires run in pairs. One wire carries electricity into the house. The other wire carries electricity out of the house. The wires run to all the *outlets* and *switches*. The outlets let you plug into the electrical power that runs through the wiring. Switches stop and start the flow of the electricity.

The electricity runs through the wires to the object that is plugged in. It turns the object on and makes it work. The electricity then runs from the object back through the wires. It flows back to the transformer, into the power lines, and back to the generator at the power plant. The round-trip takes less than a second!

Electricity

How does electricity flow through our houses?

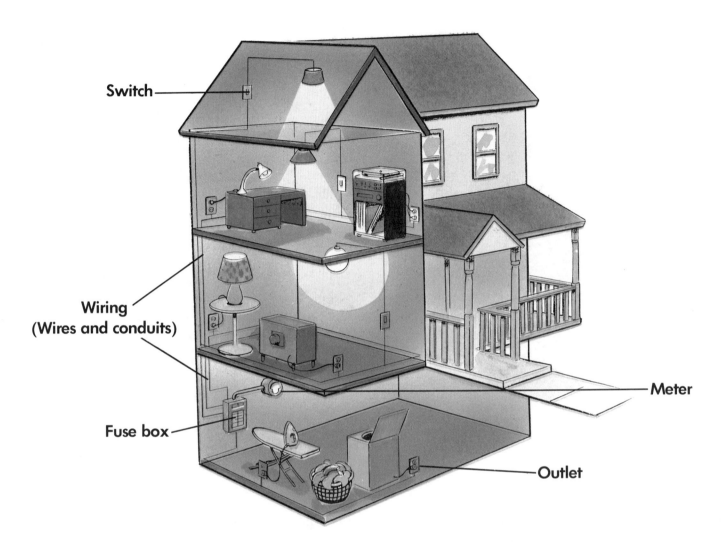

Switch

Wiring (Wires and conduits)

Fuse box

Meter

Outlet

Electricity runs through a *circuit*. (A circuit is a loop.) You make a circuit when you plug a lamp cord into a wall **outlet** and flip a **switch**. Flipping a wall switch stops and starts the electricity from flowing through the circuit.

Electricity comes into your house through the **meter**. From there, it passes through a **fuse** (or circuit breaker) **box**. Fuses (and circuit breakers) keep the wires from getting too hot. If the wires get too hot, they can be dangerous. If a wire becomes dangerous, the fuse (or circuit breaker) stops the flow of electricity until the problem is fixed.

Electrical wires run through your house inside a thin pipe. The pipe is the **conduit** (KAHN-doo-it). The conduit leads the wires to each outlet and switch in your house. The electricity is ready to use.

Let's take the example of a lamp. As you push the plug into an outlet, you are adding a piece to the circuit. Electricity flows out of the outlet and through the cord. Flip the lamp switch on and electricity runs through a thin wire inside the light bulb. This wire glows brightly when electricity heats it. The lamp gives off light.

Walkie-talkie

How do walkie-talkies talk to each other?

Walkie-talkies *transmit*, or send, and *receive*, or get, radio signals. Radio signals can go through anything—but metal. With a walkie-talkie, you can sit in your room and talk to someone in another house. Walkie-talkies run on batteries and can be carried.

To transmit a message, you talk into the **mouthpiece**. The mouthpiece has a microphone. To send a message, you press the **switch**. Pressing in the switch sends the message from the mouthpiece to the **antenna**.

As you speak into the microphone, it changes your message into voice signals. An **amplifier** makes the voice signals louder. A **modulator** changes these loud voice signals into radio signals. The radio signals then go through a **signal booster**. The booster makes the signals stronger. Signals leave the walkie-talkie through the antenna. From there, the radio signals travel in waves through the air. The voice message has been transmitted.

When the radio signals hit the **antenna** of another walkie-talkie, they travel down into the walkie-talkie. To receive a message, you stop pressing the **switch**. Letting out the switch sends the message from the antenna to the **earpiece**. The **demodulator** changes the radio signals back into sound signals. An **amplifier** makes the sound signals stronger, then sends them through the speaker in the earpiece. The speaker changes the signals back into sound. The voice message has been received.

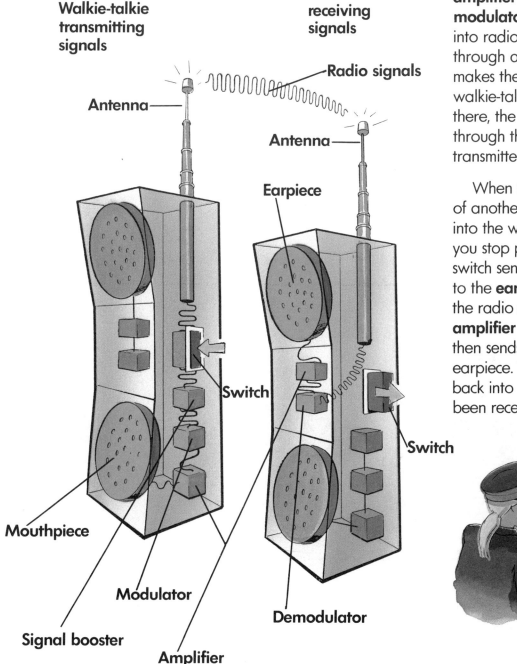

Walkie-talkie transmitting signals

Walkie-talkie receiving signals

Radio signals

Antenna

Antenna

Earpiece

Switch

Switch

Mouthpiece

Modulator

Demodulator

Signal booster

Amplifier

Submarine

How can submarines stay underwater for so long?

The long, smooth shape of the submarine is perfect for gliding through the ocean. The **hull** of the sub is a double wall. The hull stands up to high *pressure*. The pressure of the deep water—the pushing of the water against the walls of the submarine—can be very strong. A **propeller** moves the sub through the water. **Fins** and **rudders** steer the sub through the water.

Between the double walls of the hull are **ballast** (BAL-uhst) **chambers**. When the chambers fill with water, the submarine gets heavier. As the sub gets heavier, it sinks lower—it is *submerged*. Compressed air moves the water out of the chambers. (Compressed air is air that has been squeezed to fit into a smaller space.) As the submarine gets lighter, it rises.

A **conning tower** lets the crew see above the water while the sub is still underwater. This raised tower sits on top of the hull. It holds a **periscope**, radar equipment, and radio antennas. This equipment lets sailors know where they are and where they are going. They help the sailors command the sub. The conning tower, then, is a command center.

The nuclear (NYOO-klee-ur) submarine runs on *nuclear power*. The **nuclear reactor** creates steam. The steam turns the **power turbine** (TUR-buhn). The turbine makes the generators run. The generators make electricity.

Electricity does many things. It makes oxygen from sea water for the sailors to

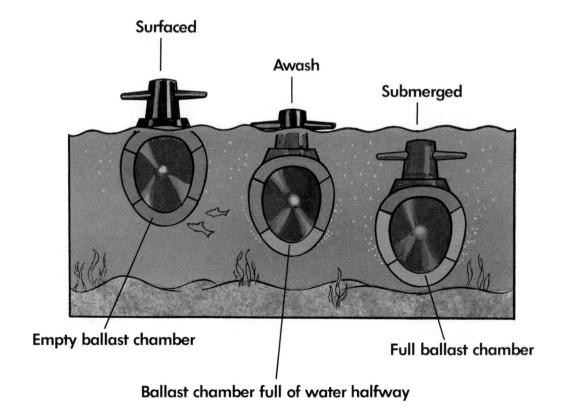

Surfaced

Awash

Submerged

Empty ballast chamber

Ballast chamber full of water halfway

Full ballast chamber

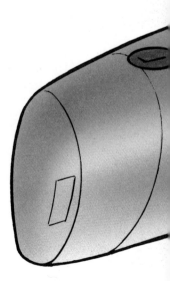

breathe. It runs the lights in the **dining area** and the **crew's quarters**. The sailors eat their meals in the dining area. The sailors sleep and dress in the crew's quarters. Electricity also runs the motor that makes the propeller spin.

A nuclear submarine does not *surface* (come above water) until its fuel needs refilling. The nuclear submarines of the United States can travel about 400,000 miles before refueling.

The first submarine was built by Cornelius Van Drebbel in 1615. Made of wood and leather, it was rowed underwater like a rowboat.

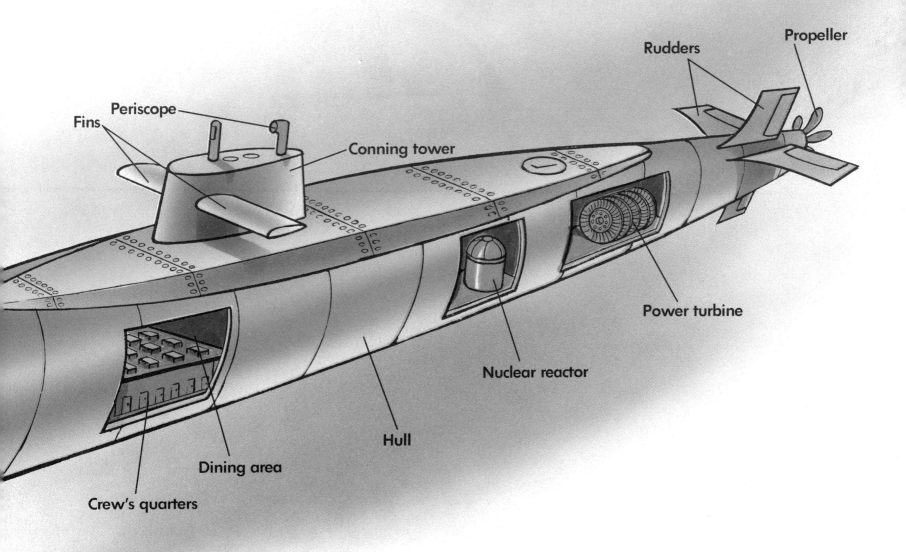

Fins

Periscope

Conning tower

Rudders

Propeller

Power turbine

Nuclear reactor

Hull

Dining area

Crew's quarters

Windup toy

What makes a windup toy move?

A windup toy uses a spring to store—and release—the energy that makes it work. (A spring is a thin, curled piece of metal.) When a spring is wound up, it *stores*, or keeps, energy. As the spring unwinds, it *releases*, or gives off, energy. Energy makes things move. The tighter the spring is wound, the more energy it stores.

Turning the toy's **key** winds the **mainspring**. As the mainspring is wound, a **pawl** catches in the teeth of the **ratchet wheel**. The pawl lets the ratchet wheel move in only one direction. The pawl keeps the mainspring from unwinding right away. One

end of the spring is fixed to the toy. The other **end** of the spring is fixed to the key.

Letting go of the key lets the mainspring unwind. The pawl does not hold back the ratchet wheel. The pawl clicks over the teeth of the ratchet wheel as the key turns.

As the mainspring unwinds, it moves a system of gears (more wheels with teeth). Gears make the toy's parts move.

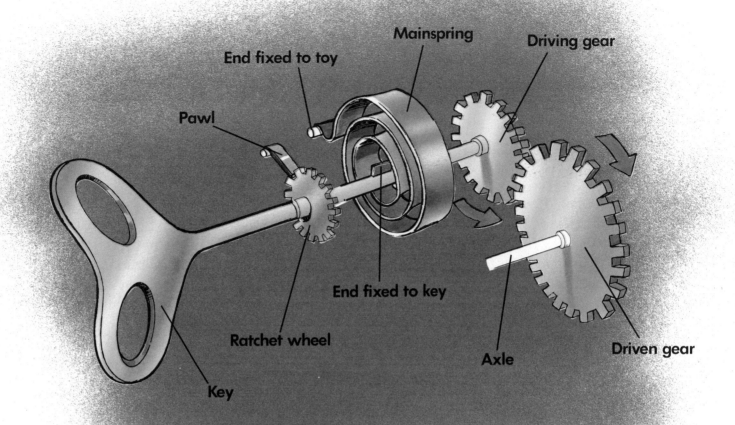

Mainspring

End fixed to toy

Driving gear

Pawl

Key

End fixed to key

Ratchet wheel

Axle

Driven gear

In a windup toy car, for example, two gears make the car's wheels turn. One gear—the **driving gear**—is attached to the key. The other gear—the **driven gear**—is attached to the **axle**. (An axle is a short rod with a wheel on each end.) The teeth of the driving gear fit into the teeth of the driven gear.

As the spring unwinds, energy moves from the spring into the driving gear. The driving gear then turns the driven gear, the driven gear turns the axle, and the axle turns the wheels. The energy keeps the gears turning into each other and the wheels moving.

43

Typewriters

How do different typewriters type?

Working the keys and paper on a **manual typewriter** is done by hand.

Pushing down on a **key** on the keyboard moves a lever. The lever pulls on a **type bar**. The type bar is a long metal strip that attaches to the key. Each type bar has two **characters** on its end.

Characters are letters, numbers, and symbols (like question marks, plus signs, and so on). For letters, a capital letter is on the top of the type bar. Its lowercase letter is beneath it. Numbers and symbols are on the type bar just as they are on the key. A symbol is on top; a number is on the bottom. The type bars are laid out in a semicircle. All

characters are raised up off the metal bar. The raised characters are reversed—they look backward. The reversed characters print facing the right way.

The lever pushes the type bar forward. The type bar hits the **ribbon**. (All the type bars strike the ribbon in the center.) The ribbon has ink on it and is stretched close to the paper. As the type bar hits the ribbon, the ribbon is pressed to the paper. The character leaves its mark on the paper. The type bar goes back to its place. Pressing the shift key moves the type bars down. The capital letters and symbols hit the ribbon. Not pressing the shift key means the type bar types lowercase letters and numbers.

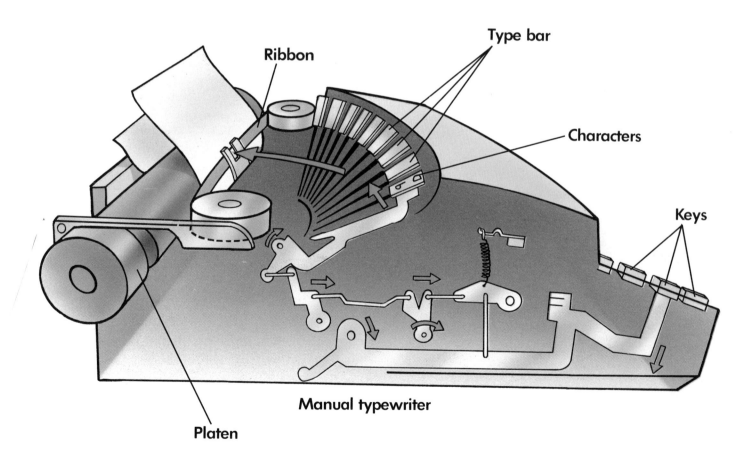

Type bar

Ribbon

Characters

Keys

Manual typewriter

Platen

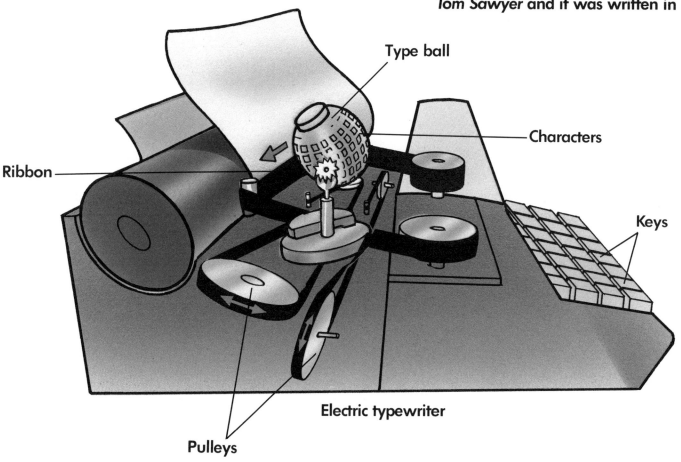

Mark Twain was the first writer to use a typewriter to write a book. The book was *Tom Sawyer* and it was written in 1875.

Type ball

Characters

Ribbon

Keys

Electric typewriter

Pulleys

The paper is fed under and around a **platen**. The platen is a roller that is covered with rubber. The platen is part of the typewriter's carriage. The carriage moves as the characters are typed. With each typed character, the carriage moves over one space. It is in position for the next character. The carriage moves across the page until it reaches the end of a line. The return lever moves the carriage back to its starting place and moves the paper up one line. The typewriter then types the next line.

An **electric typewriter** works much the same way as does a manual typewriter. The difference is that electricity does some of the work.

A motor sends electricity to the **type ball**. The type ball is a metal ball covered with characters. Again, these letters, numbers, and symbols are raised and reversed. As a key is hit, the type ball spins around for the character and tilts toward the ribbon. The type ball presses the inked ribbon to the paper. The character leaves its mark on the paper.

Pulleys move the type ball across the paper. The type ball zips back and forth in the typewriter as it types characters.

Pressing a return key sends the type ball back to the beginning of a new line and moves the paper up.

Cordless phone

How can a cordless phone make and get phone calls?

A cordless telephone is a combination of a telephone and a two-way radio. It is made up of a **base phone** and a **handset**.

The base phone runs on electricity. It plugs into the wall outlet in your home. The base phone is also connected to the telephone system. It is wired into the regular phone lines. It plugs into a phone jack in your home.

The handset can be up to 1,500 feet from the base phone and still transmit and receive messages. The handset runs on batteries. The batteries are *recharged* when the handset is hung up. (Recharging means to fill the batteries with energy.)

A radio transmitter and receiver are built into both the base phone and the handset. The transmitter and receiver run on electricity. The person talking sends signals—his or her voice—with the transmitter. The person listening gets signals—the voice—with the receiver. An **antenna** on the base phone sends signals to and gets signals from the **antenna** on the handset.

Radio signals can go through anything except metal. The cordless phone can send and get radio signals at the same time. Callers can talk and listen at the same time. Walkie-talkies can only do one thing at a time.

The first cordless phones could not be used to call people more than 1½ miles away.

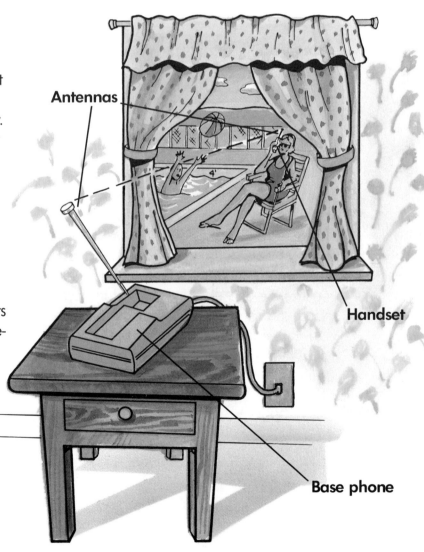

Antennas

Handset

Base phone

46

Water pistol

Why does a water pistol squirt?

A water pistol squirts because water can't be squeezed to fit into a smaller space. Try it yourself: Fill a balloon with water and squeeze it. Watch what the water does. It shifts from end to end—it doesn't get smaller.

Inside a water pistol is **water** and a **tube**. The tube has a tiny hole in the end. A **piston** fits inside the tube. (A piston is a plug that slides back and forth.) A **spring** connects the piston and the **trigger**. Squeezing the trigger pushes the piston forward. The piston moves toward the hole. Letting go of the trigger moves the piston back.

The tube has another hole. It is in the top of the tube. This hole lets water into the tube when the piston is pulled back. Water fills the tube. Squeeze the trigger and the piston pushes the water through the hole in the end of the pistol. The water has only one place to go—it must go out.

The piston is about 100 times bigger than the little hole in the end of the pistol. When the piston pushes forward, the water must go through the hole 100 times faster than the piston is pushing. This high speed makes a hard, thin stream of water. The water pistol squirts!

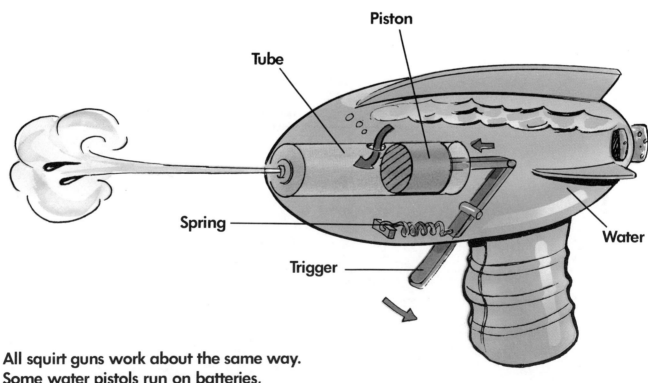

All squirt guns work about the same way. Some water pistols run on batteries, though, and can squirt water fast and far. These pistols are often big and hold a lot of water. Some water pistols even have lights and sound effects. These pistols look and sound like space guns.

Magic tricks

How does a magician saw a person in half?

Most magic tricks work by *misdirection*. To be misdirected is to give your attention to another place. A magician will have the audience pay attention to something else while the trick is taking place. When a magician pulls a rabbit out of a hat, the magician waves the wand. We are watching this "show" instead of noticing that the assistant is putting a rabbit into the hat!

Magic tricks also work because people see what they *expect* to see—whether it is there or not. Would you ever think to count the fingers on a magician's hands? We see ten fingers because we expect to see ten fingers. A place for a magician to hide a silk scarf is in a hollow fake finger. If the magician does not draw our attention to it, we never see it. Presto! A scarf is pulled out of the air!

A favorite magic trick is **sawing a person in half**. The magician and the assistant perform this trick together. The assistant first climbs into a **large box** that is resting on a **table.** The box has **holes on each end**. One end has a hole for the assistant's head and hands. The other end has holes for the assistant's feet.

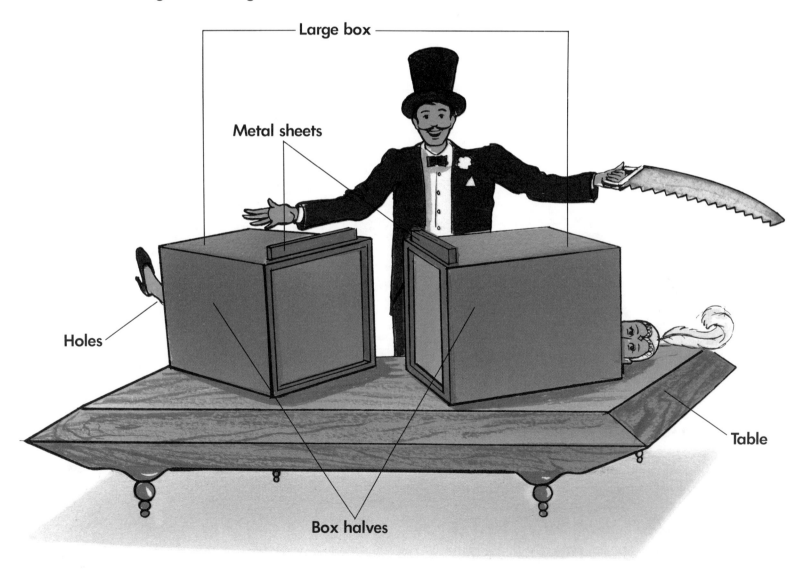

Large box

Metal sheets

Holes

Table

Box halves

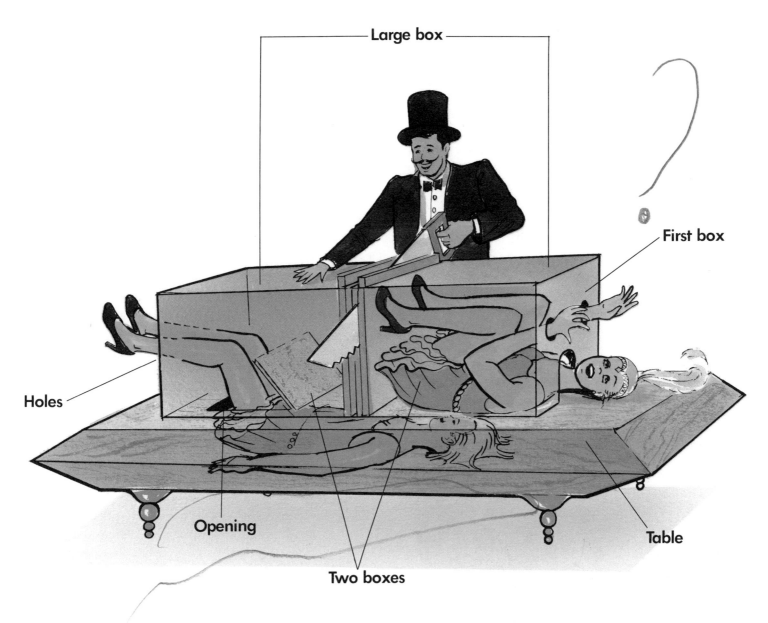

Large box

First box

Holes

Opening

Table

Two boxes

The magician then saws the box—and the assistant—in half. When the magician finishes sawing, **two metal sheets** are slipped between the two halves of the box. The **halves of the box** are pushed apart. The assistant is cut in half!

The magician pushes the two halves together again and takes out the metal sheets. The assistant climbs out in one piece! Is it magic?

It is not magic. It is just that we expect the feet, head, and hands belong to one assistant. Two assistants help the magician do this trick.

One assistant climbs into the **large box**. The other assistant hides inside the **table**. The box is really **two boxes** in one. One box

is the box that the assistant climbs into. It has a bottom built into it. The other box is for the hidden assistant. The hidden assistant's legs and feet go through this box. It has a top built into it. It also has an **opening** for the assistant's legs and feet.

The hidden assistant's legs push through the opening in the second box and the assistant's feet stick out of the **holes** on the end. It looks as if the assistant climbing into the box is the one whose feet are sticking through the holes. The legs of the assistant climbing into the box are tucked in to fit into the **first box**.

The saw never touches either assistant. The sheets of metal hide the bottom and top of the two boxes when the halves are pulled apart.

49

Magic tricks

How does a magician make a scarf disappear?

The **disappearing scarf** is another popular magic trick. The magician stuffs the scarf into either hand. The magician opens both hands and they are empty!

A magician makes a scarf disappear by using a **pull**. (A pull is a small cup attached to a long, strong rubber band.) **One end of the rubber band** is attached to the back of the magician's **belt**. The **other end of the rubber band** is attached to the **cup**. The cup is pulled around and tucked into the magician's belt at the side. The magician's **cape** hides the pull.

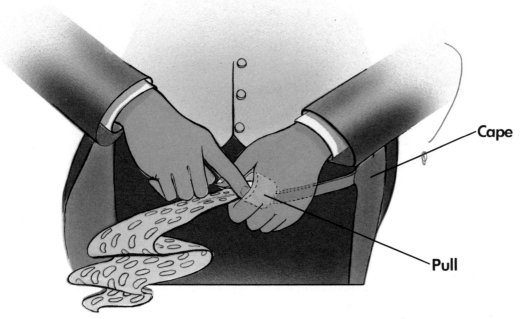

Cape

Pull

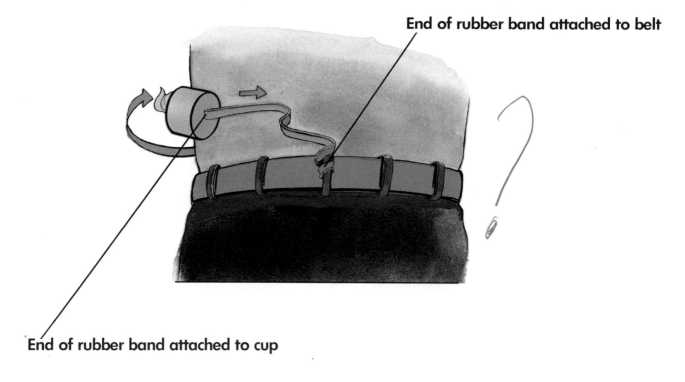

End of rubber band attached to belt

End of rubber band attached to cup

While the audience is listening to the magician talk and watching the magician's arms wave, the magician takes the cup in one hand. The audience does not know it is there.

The magician stuffs the scarf into the cup in the hand. The magician lets go of the cup and the rubber band pulls it around. While the audience is listening to the magician's magic words and watching the magician's hands, the cup—stuffed with the scarf—zips behind the magician.

Automatic door

How do doors open and close automatically?

Doors that open *automatically* (aht-uh-MAT-i-klee), or on their own, are handy and save time.

Some automatic doors sense that you are there. They "see" you with many electronic eyes. One part of each eye sends out a beam of light. The light is invisible to your eye. The light shines across the doorway.

The other part of each eye "watches" the beam of light. When you step into the beam, you stop the light from reaching the eye. The blocked light is a signal to open the door. Electricity opens and closes the door. As long as the eye sees the beam, the door stays closed.

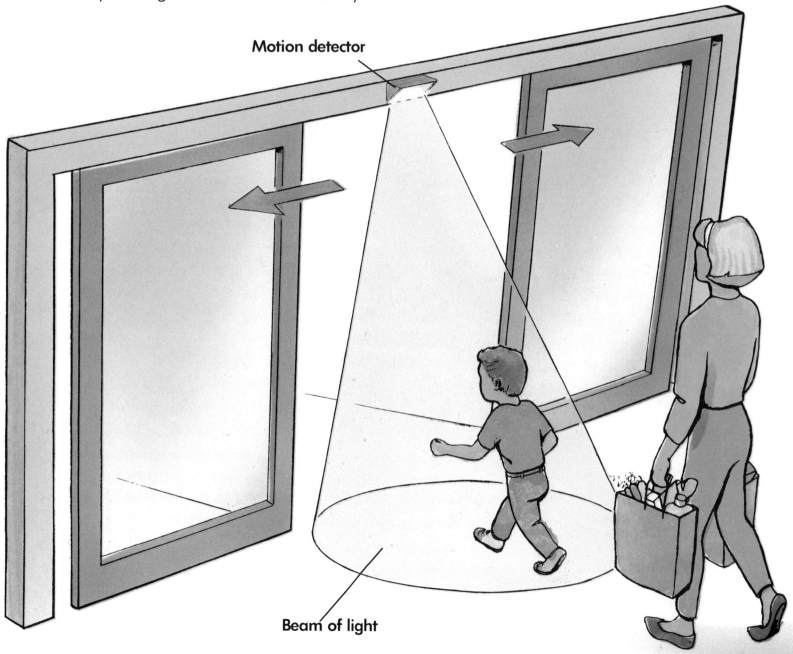

Motion detector

Beam of light

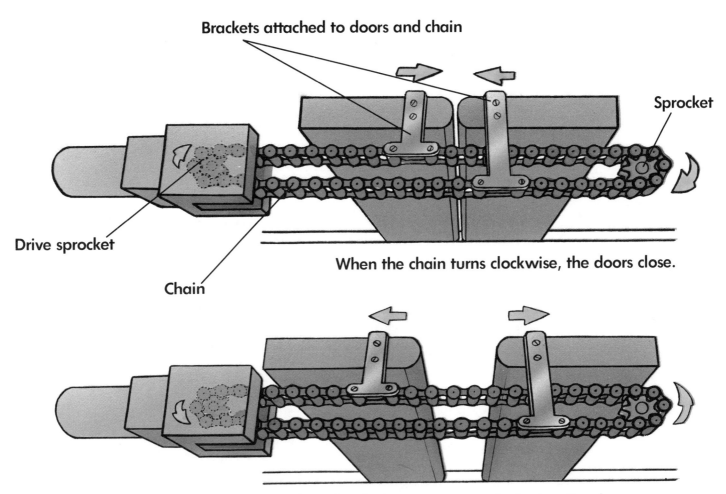

Brackets attached to doors and chain

Sprocket

Drive sprocket

Chain

When the chain turns clockwise, the doors close.

When the chain turns counterclockwise, the doors open.

Other automatic doors can sense you are nearing the door. This time, the "eye" is a **motion detector.** The detector picks up nearby movement. It is placed over the door. It watches a **beam of invisible light** that shines on the floor. When you step into the pool of light, you change the signal. The sensor sees the change and opens the door. When there is no movement, the doors stay closed.

Some automatic doors don't use electronic eyes. Elevator doors open with the push of a button. The rubber mat in front of some supermarket doors is like a giant push button. These doors open electrically. Electricity opens and closes the doors. A timer holds the door open for a few seconds so you can pass through.

Automatic doors open in different ways. They can swing open. Doors in a home swing open. They also can slide into the wall. Elevator doors slide into the wall.

The swinging door has a motor with an "arm." The arm is fixed to the top of the door. As the motor turns, it moves the arm. As the arm moves, it opens the door.

On sliding doors, a motor turns a **drive sprocket**. (A sprocket is a wheel with pointy teeth.) **Brackets** connect a **chain** to each door. The sprocket's teeth fit into a chain the same way the gear teeth of a bicycle fit into a bike chain. The chain moves around another **sprocket** on the opposite end of the drive sprocket. As the motor turns, the chain pulls the doors open. The sprocket reverses to close the doors.

Albert Einstein came up with the idea for the electronic eye in 1921. Later, other scientists made an invention using his research to help them. Today, some electronic eyes can "see" such fast-moving objects as a bullet in flight.

Etch A Sketch drawing board

How does an Etch A Sketch drawing board draw?

1. The Etch A Sketch drawing board has a **screen**.

2. The screen is set into a **box**. The box is not deep. Inside the box, under the screen, is aluminum powder. The powder is like dust. Small plastic beads inside the box keep the aluminum powdery. Turning the box over and shaking it makes the beads spread the powder over the inside of the screen. When the box is turned right-side up again, a thin layer of powder sticks to the glass. The screen looks silver.

3. **Two knobs** on the top of the box are connected to tiny pulleys inside the board. (A pulley is a wheel with a groove. The groove holds a long string.) Twisting the knobs makes the pulleys turn.

4. **Two loops of string** pass over each pulley.

5. Each of the loops of string is connected to one end of a wire. The wires hold the **rods.**

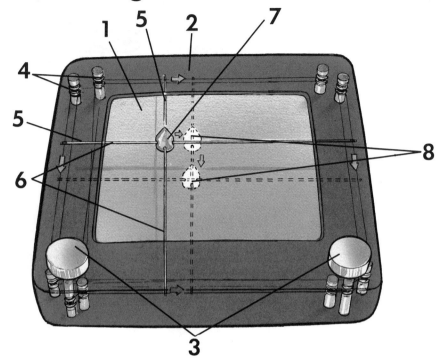

6. The left knob moves a **rod** that runs from the top to the bottom of the drawing board. The right knob moves a **rod** that runs from side to side. The two rods cross each other.

7. A small metal ring marks where the rods cross. On the ring is a **plastic point**. The plastic point presses against the inside of the glass screen.

8. When the left knob turns, the plastic point moves **left and right** across the screen. When the right knob turns, the plastic point moves **up and down** the screen.

   Wherever the plastic point goes, it rubs the aluminum powder from the inside of the screen. Everywhere the powder is rubbed off the glass becomes see-through. Because the inside of the box is dark, darkness comes through the line that was drawn. The lines show up as dark lines on the silver screen.

LP record

How does a record play music?

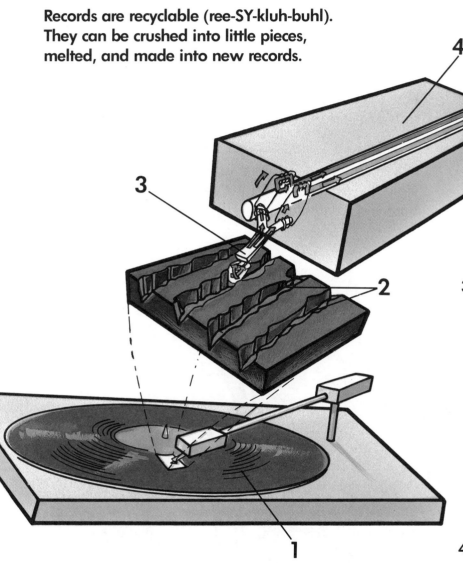

3. A **phonograph needle** rides in the groove. As the record player's motor spins the record 33⅓ times a minute, the needle moves through the groove. As the needle moves along, the bumps in the sides of the groove push it back and forth. The bumps make the needle *vibrate*. (To vibrate is to move back and forth.)

   The **bumps** make the same pattern as the sounds made when they were recorded. The vibrations of the needle match the vibrations of the sound.

4. The vibrations run through the needle and into a **cartridge.** Inside the cartridge is a transducer. The transducer turns the vibrations into electrical signals. These signals match the pattern of the original music.

   The signals then go to an amplifier. The amplifier makes the signals louder.

   The loudspeakers change the signals back into the music that we hear.

1. An LP (*long-playing*) record is a disk with one long, narrow **groove**. The groove spirals, or winds, around and around. It winds from the outside edge to the middle of the record.

2. Although they are invisible to the eye, the **sides of the groove** are bumpy.

Stringed instruments

How does a stringed instrument make music?

A musician has to do two things to play a stringed instrument. The musician must set one or more of the strings into motion. Plucking the string with a finger or drawing a bow across the string makes it move. And the musician must control the amount of string that moves. Pressing the string with a finger controls the amount of string that moves.

Each kind of stringed instrument makes a different kind of sound. Some sound like deep growls; some sound like sweet songs. An instrument's sound depends on many things. Its size and shape, the material of which it is made, the kind of strings it has, how it is played, and more all affect the sound an instrument makes.

A **violin** is explained here. Other instruments that look like a violin are the **viola**, the **violoncello** (or just **cello**), and the **bass viol** (or just **bass**).

Bass

Viola

Violin

Cello

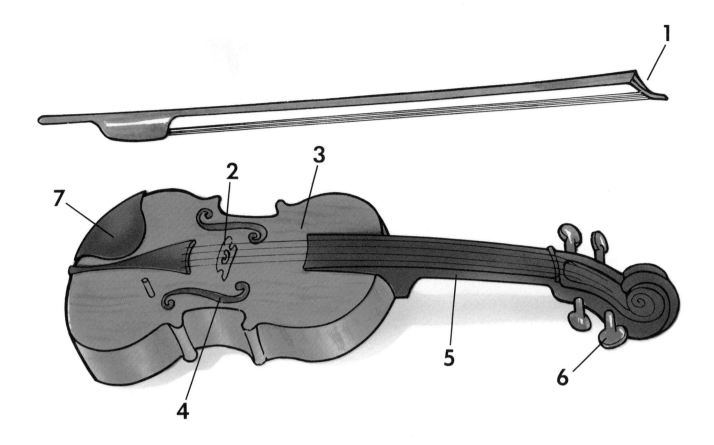

1. A violin is played by drawing a **bow** across its four strings. The bow is strung with horsehair. As the bow string rubs against the string of the violin, the violin string moves back and forth. It *vibrates*.

2. The four **strings** of the violin are stretched over a curved **bridge**.

3. The vibration of the string is made louder by the body of the violin. The vibration of the string travels through the bridge and into the **soundboard**. The soundboard is the wooden top of the violin. A post connects the soundboard to the back of the violin. Both the soundboard and the back of the violin vibrate with the string. The violin's front and back are much bigger than the string—they make the vibration loud enough to hear.

4. The sound comes out through **holes** in the top of the violin. The sound of the string depends on how long it is and how tight it is. The shorter the string is, the higher the sound. The tighter the string is, the higher the sound.

5. By **pressing a string against the neck**, the violinist only allows part of the string to vibrate. Moving the fingers up and down the neck changes the amount of string that can vibrate.

   Pressing a finger to the neck of the violin shortens the amount of string that can vibrate. The shortened string makes a high sound. The highest notes that can be heard vibrate about 20,000 times a second.

   Not pressing a finger to the neck of the violin keeps the amount of string that can vibrate long. The long string makes a low sound. The lowest notes that can be heard vibrate about 20 times a second.

6. Each string is wound around a **peg** in the **pegbox**. The pegbox is at the end of the neck. Turning the pegs to tighten or loosen the strings *tunes* the strings. Tuning an instrument means the strings make the right sounds. Tightening shortens the string. Loosening lengthens the string.

Maglev

How does a maglev travel across tracks?

A "maglev" is a "*magnetically levitated* train." *Magnetically* (mag-NET-i-klee) means "with a magnet." *Levitate* (LEV-uh-tayt) means to "to rise" or "to float." A magnetically levitated train is a train that uses a magnet to rise off a track.

A maglev runs on a **guideway**. Guideways are tracks made of concrete and steel. The tracks are lined with **electromagnets**. The magnets on the tracks work with **electromagnets** on the train to lift the train off the track. (An electromagnet is a core, or center, of metal. Wire is wound around the core. Electricity running through the wire turns the core into a magnet. Electromagnets can be very powerful.) The maglev rides along on a cushion of air.

The **flange** (flanj) on each side of the maglev wraps around the track. The flange is the bottom of the train. Electromagnets line the inside of each flange. Batteries on the train power the magnets on the track. The magnets on the track pull the lower lip of the flange toward the track.

A computer measures the distance between the electromagnets and the track—the cushion of air the train runs on must be the same all along the track.

Alignment (uh-LYN-muhnt) **magnets** sit on the sides of the flange. They keep the train running straight along the track.

The magnets along the side of the guideway pull the train along the tracks. The electricity that runs through the track's electromagnets flows very fast. As the electricity flows through each magnet along the track, that magnet pulls the train toward it. As the magnets pull the train, the train makes its way down the track.

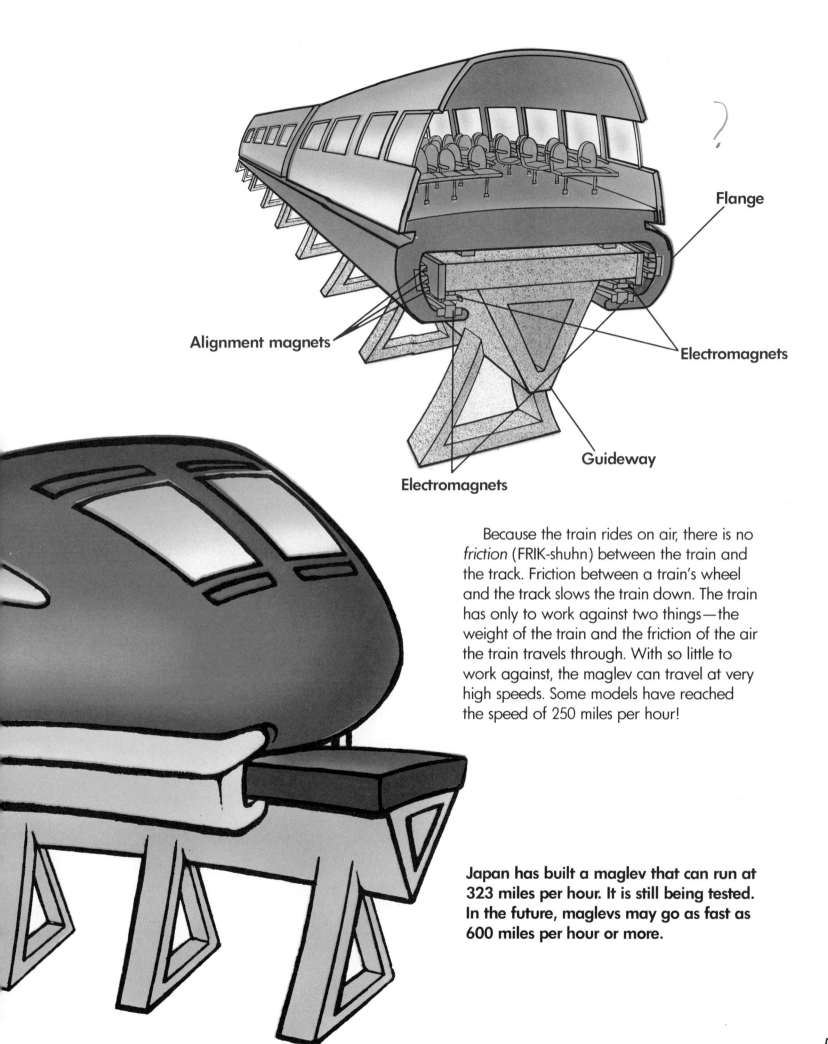

Flange

Alignment magnets

Electromagnets

Guideway

Electromagnets

Because the train rides on air, there is no *friction* (FRIK-shuhn) between the train and the track. Friction between a train's wheel and the track slows the train down. The train has only to work against two things—the weight of the train and the friction of the air the train travels through. With so little to work against, the maglev can travel at very high speeds. Some models have reached the speed of 250 miles per hour!

Japan has built a maglev that can run at 323 miles per hour. It is still being tested. In the future, maglevs may go as fast as 600 miles per hour or more.

Skateboard

How is a skateboard able to ride around and do turns?

A skateboard, or deck, is a board with two **axles**. (The axles are rods with a wheel on each end.) **Trucks** attach the axles to the board. (Trucks are T-shaped metal pieces.) Trucks let the rider steer.

When the rider presses down on one side of the board with a foot, the part of the truck that holds the axle turns a little. Because the trucks turn, the wheels can turn. Each wheel spins by itself. The skateboard goes in the direction of the pressure.

The truck acts like a *hinge*. (A hinge is a metal piece that lets things move. A hinge lets a swinging door swing, for example.) The truck hinges on two points. One point is the pin at one end of the truck. The other point is the ring on the other end of the truck. A **bolt** goes through the ring. (A bolt is like a short rod. A **nut** screws on the end of the bolt. A bolt and nut are used to fasten things together.) The bolt connects the ring to the truck. Thick **rubber rings** fit between the bolt and the ring. Making the nut looser or tighter makes turning easier.

When the rider presses down on the board, the truck and the axle bend toward the side being pressed down. When the rider lets up on the pressure, the rubber rings push the truck back into place.

If the truck were like a regular hinge, the wheels would just move toward the board when the rider pressed down on the side. Because the pin sits closer to the board than the ring sits, the truck bends toward the board and in the direction of the ring. Because the bolt faces the center of the board, the wheels under pressure move toward the center of the board. The outside wheels move toward the sides of the board. The skateboard goes into a turn.

Many top skateboarders today perform spins and jumps on U-shaped wooden ramps. Their boards may have plastic rings on the T-shaped part of the truck. Plastic rings don't let the trucks move around as much as rubber rings do. To turn, the rider pushes down with his or her back foot rather than pushing down on one side of the board. The front of the board lifts off the ground. The board spins around on its back wheels. The **tail** turns up at the end for kick turns.

The best skateboarders use the **rails** on the bottom of the board to turn. The rails are the handholds. To do this, the rider jumps off the ground, grabs the rails, and spins the board around.

Rubber or plastic rings

Truck

Nut

Axle

Bolt

Rail

Tail

61

Hook-and-loop fastener

How does a hook-and-loop fastener stick together?

A hook-and-loop fastener is made of two pieces of tape. One piece of tape holds the **hooks**. The other piece of tape holds the **loops**.

The hooks are really threads that are sewn into the tape. The threads are made of *nylon*. Nylon is a strong material. The nylon threads are sewn into the tape in many tiny loops. The loops are then cut open to make tiny hooks.

The second half of the fastener—the loops—is made the same way. The loops also are made of nylon that has been fixed to a tape backing. Fluffy fibers, not regular loops, are sewn in. The hooks stick to these fibers.

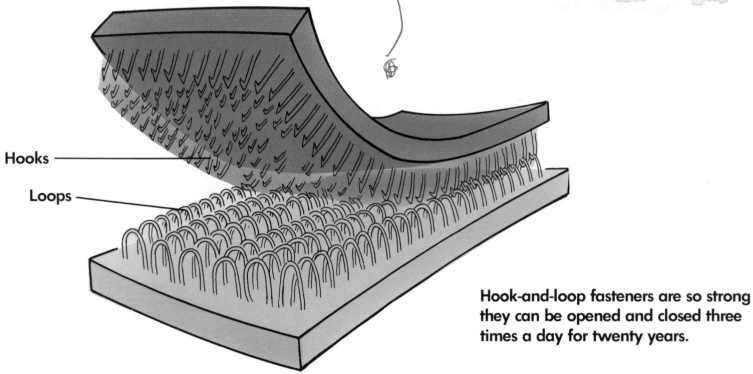

Hooks

Loops

Hook-and-loop fasteners are so strong they can be opened and closed three times a day for twenty years.

Pen

How does a pen write?

A pen writes by putting ink to paper. The ink dries very fast.

A common pen is the ball-point pen. A plastic **casing** holds the ball-point pen together. **Ink** flows through a **tube** inside the casing. One end of the tube is a **socket**. The socket holds a tiny rolling **ball**. As the ball rolls, it becomes coated with ink. The ink is then rolled onto the paper.

Quill pens of long ago were made of goose, swan, or crow feathers. The inside of these feathers was hollow. The core, or tip, could hold a little ink. The feather stem was split and carved to a point. Ink would flow from inside the feather to the core. The core scratched ink against the paper. The quill was dipped into an inkwell to soak up more ink into its core. Today quill pens are called fountain pens. They have a supply of ink flowing through them.

A felt-tipped pen is a cross between a fountain pen and a paintbrush. The felt tip is soaked with ink that is like a fast-drying paint. When the felt tip rubs against the paper, it "paints" a line.

The ball-point pen was announced as being the first pen that could write underwater. To get people to buy the pen, one store had some people sit in tanks filled with water and write with the pens. The tanks were put in the store's windows. That day, almost 10,000 ball-point pens were sold.

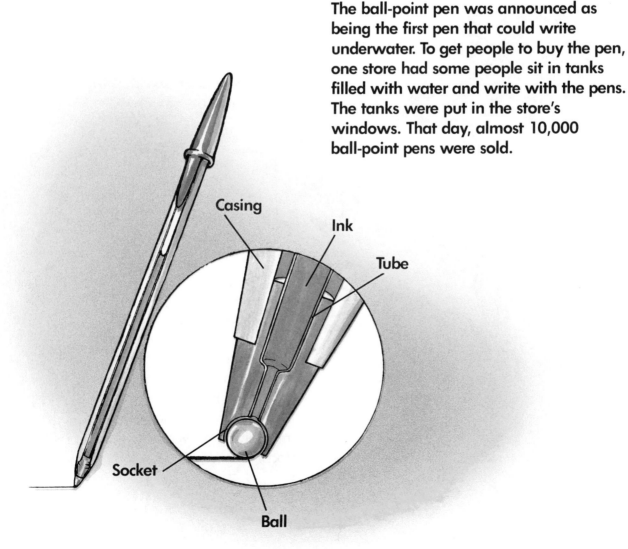

Casing

Ink

Tube

Socket

Ball

Microscope

How does a microscope magnify things that are so small they are invisible to the eye?

A compound microscope uses more than one lens to magnify the image of an invisible object.

Our eyes cannot *focus* on, or clearly see, things that are very close. Try it yourself: Hold a coin an inch from your right eye while the left one is closed. The coin is blurry. Slowly move the coin away from your eye. It becomes clear.

The part of the eye on which the image is seen is the *retina* (RET-i-nuh). (The retina is like a movie screen on the back wall of the eyeball.) Holding something close to your eye makes the image on the retina big. But the angle at which the light from the object comes into the eye is still too small. The eye cannot focus on the image.

A magnifying glass bends the light waves from the object's image. The image is made bigger before it reaches the retina of the eye. The eye focuses on the image.

The lens of a magnifying glass is *converging* (kahn-VUR-jing). Converging means that the glass bends light rays so they

When an object is within the focal length of the lens, the object looks bigger.

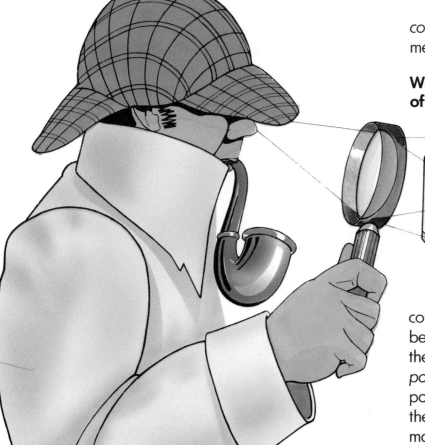

come together at a point, which appears to be farther away than it would be without the magnifying glass. That point is the *focal point*. When the object is between the focal point and the lens, its image looks bigger in the lens. The distance between the magnifying glass and the focal point is the *focal length*.

A microscope has many parts to it. It needs all these parts to work.

1. There first must be enough **light** to see the object.

2. Light—daylight or electric—is pointed up into the microscope by a **mirror**. A lens above the mirror is *adjustable*. The mirror can be moved to change the amount of light that comes into the microscope.

3. Because the object to be looked at must let the light pass through it, it is sliced very thin. This slice is a sample of the object. The sample is a **specimen** (SPES-i-men). The specimen is placed on a clear **glass slide**.

4. The **platform** has clips to hold the slide in place.

5. The light shines through the specimen and into the **objective lens**. The objective lens is the first lens. The image is *enlarged*, or made bigger. The image can be twenty times bigger than the size of the object.

6. Microscopes often have several objective lenses. By turning the **turret**, you can choose objectives that will make the image up to 100 times the size of the object.

7. After the image is made bigger by the objective, it goes to the **ocular** (AHK-yu-lahr) **lens**. The ocular lens is the eyepiece. You look at the slide through the ocular lens. It can enlarge the image by ten times. The image you would then see through the eyepiece would be 200 times bigger than the real specimen (20 x 10 = 200)!

8. The **focusing knob** makes the distance between the objective lens and the ocular lens bigger and smaller. Your eye can then see the image clearly.

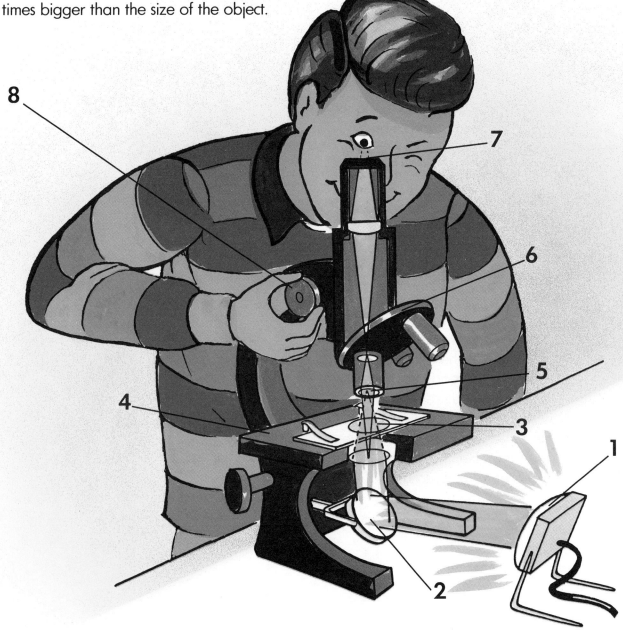

65

Stereophonic sound

Why does stereophonic sound seem to come from all directions?

The sounds you hear every day come at you from all directions. A sound not only comes straight from the *source*. (The source is the thing that makes the sound.) A sound can bounce off a wall or a ceiling. Sound coming out of one speaker, like that from a radio, is flat. The sound comes from only one direction. It does not sound like the sounds you hear every day. Sound coming out of a stereo—called stereophonic (ster-ee-uh-FAHN-ik) sound—seems to come from many directions.

More than one microphone—usually many more—is used to record stereo sound. The microphones are placed where the best recording can be made. This can be to the sides of a band, on either side of an instrument—anywhere. Each microphone picks up a sound that is a little different from the sound another microphone picks up. Each recording adds to the stereo effect of the sound because each microphone picks up a different sound. The sounds are recorded onto separate tapes. These tapes are sound tracks. More than 20 tracks may be used to record a band playing.

The tracks all come together to make the recording. Listening to the recording sounds as if the band were spread out behind the loudspeakers. The sound seems to bounce all over. Some of the tracks come out of one loudspeaker. Others will come out of the other speaker. Together, the sounds will be just as they are at a live concert.

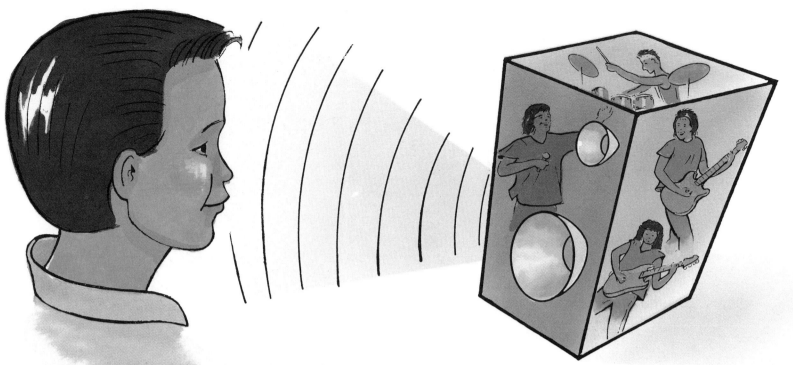

Different things can be done when the sound is being recorded. Some instruments can be recorded on only one of the sound tracks. Other instruments can be switched between the tracks. It sounds as if the instrument were moving around the room.

Listening to sound through headphones is really listening to two separate speakers. A different sound comes out of each earpiece of the headphones. The two sounds come together. When they come together, they sound real.

The Walt Disney film *Fantasia* played in stereophonic sound. It was made in 1940.

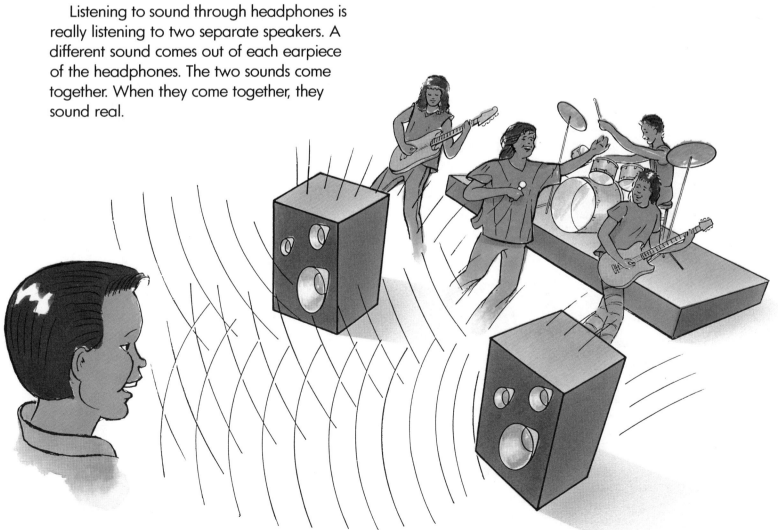

Food processor

How can a food processor chop, mix, blend, and slice all in one machine?

A food processor is one machine that can chop, mix, blend, and slice because it uses different blades for each action. A **motor** turns the blades. The blades spin inside a **covered work bowl**.

A steel knife-blade chops, mixes, and blends. The knife has two S-shaped blades. One blade spins near the bottom of the bowl, and the other spins half an inch higher. The bottom blade chops up the food. The top blade chops food and mixes or blends it.

Discs slice and shred. (Shredding means to cut into long, thin strips.) Discs are thin, flat plates. They have slots with sharp edges.

Feed tube

Work bowl

On/off switch

Motor

Safety switch

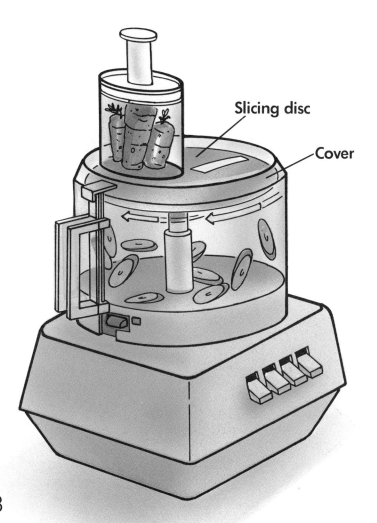

Slicing disc

Cover

A disc with long slots cuts vegetables and meats into thin slices. A disc with short slots shreds lettuce, cheese, and carrots.

To slice a carrot, the cook places it into the **feed tube** of the processor. The cook then switches on the power. As each slot passes the feed tube, it slices off one piece of the carrot. Because the disc spins so fast, it can cut up a whole carrot in seconds.

A food processor has been built so that it is safe to use. The cover locks onto the bowl and the bowl locks onto the processor. They won't fly off while the processor is running. A **safety switch** turns off the power if the bowl or lid comes unlocked.

Talking toy

How does a toy talk?

Many talking toys have little record players inside them. The sentences the toys say are recorded on a tiny record.

Pulling the **string** starts the **record**. The string wraps around a **pulley**. (A pulley is a wheel with a groove. The string fits in this groove.) Pulling the string turns the pulley. A **spring** and another pulley connect this pulley to the record.

The string is threaded through a thin tube, too. The tube connects to a **phonograph needle**. Pulling the string lifts the needle up. Letting go of the string sets the needle down on the record.

As the spring unwinds, it turns the record. The needle slides into one of the grooves on the record. It follows the path of the groove. The side of the groove has tiny bumps. The bumps make the needle move back and forth. The needle *vibrates*. The bumps of the groove match the bumps of the recording.

The top of the needle presses against a cone-shaped **speaker**. The cone changes the needle's vibrations into sound that we can understand. A **brake** makes the record play at just the right speed.

Speaker

String

Phonograph needle

Record

Spring

Brake

Pulley

69

Fireworks

What makes fireworks explode into bright colors?

Gunpowder makes fireworks explode. Gunpowder is a black powder mixture of sulphur (SUHL-fuhr), potassium nitrate (puh-TAS-ee-uhm NY-trayt), and charcoal (CHAR-kol). Gunpowder burns and explodes.

The colors that fireworks flash come from metals. Metals burn different colors. Iron (EYE-urn) burns the color of gold; barium (BAYR-ee-uhm) burns green. The metals are made into a powder. The powdered metals are then made into pellets. (Pellets look like small bullets.) The pellets in a firework are called stars. The stars are packed in the shell (or tube) of the firework.

The shells are loaded by professionals into launching tubes. The fuse is lit. (The fuse is long. The person has time to move away from the firework.)

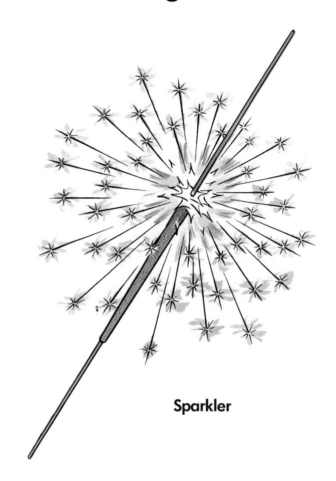

Sparkler

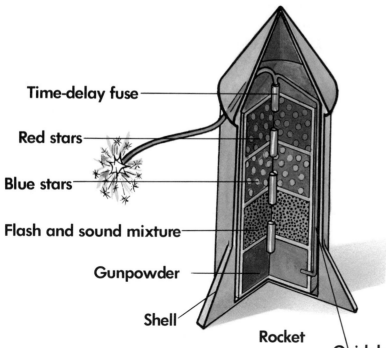

Time-delay fuse

Red stars

Blue stars

Flash and sound mixture

Gunpowder

Shell

Rocket

Quick-burning fuse

A **rocket** is one kind of firework. Its **shell** has four levels of stars and gunpowder. A **quick-burning fuse** lights both ends of the rocket at the same time. The bottom layer—the layer of **gunpowder**—is lit first. It explodes and sends the shell into the sky.

A **time-delay fuse** explodes each of the other three levels. As each level explodes, it creates colors. The top level explodes high in the sky. This level is made of more gunpowder and **red stars**. A time-delay fuse lights the next level a few seconds later. This level has **blue stars**. Another time-delay fuse lights the **flash and sound mixture**. The sound and flash mixture is made of *aluminum*. It is the aluminum that makes the bright white light and loud noise.

Sparklers are another kind of firework. A sparkler is made by dipping a wire into a "soup" of gunpowder and a *binder*. (The binder holds the gunpowder on the wire.) Mixed into the soup might be one of the powdered metals that burn in color. The mixture dries and hardens on the wire. Then the wire is dipped in aluminum. The gunpowder mixture burns, the aluminum makes sparks, and the metals make colors.

Fireworks can be dangerous. A shell could explode too early or fall back to Earth to explode. A sparkler could start a fire on the grass if it is not burned out. In the United States, people who shoot fireworks must have permission to do so. These are often people such as fire fighters. They wear protective clothing and goggles when they set off fireworks. A fire truck and ambulance stand by in case of danger.

Locks

How do locks open and close?

The pin-tumbler lock and the combination lock work in different ways.

The **pin-tumbler lock** uses a **cylinder** and **pins**. (A cylinder is a tube.) A row of pins connects the cylinder to the lock. The pins slide up and down. **Springs** push the pins down. The pins fit into holes in the cylinder. When the correct key is out of the cylinder, the pins keep the cylinder from being turned. They also keep other keys from opening the lock.

Each pin is in two pieces: The break between the pieces is different for each pin. The break does not make a straight line. It has high points and low points. Each key's **peaks** (the high points) and **valleys** (the low points) match only its lock. Only one key shape fits into the lock. When the right key is pushed into a lock, the peaks and valleys push each pin up just that amount. The break in each pin lines up exactly with the top of the cylinder. The cylinder can now be turned. The lock is unlocked.

If the wrong key is pushed into the cylinder, some—but not all—of the pins may be pushed up. If even one pin is not lined up exactly with the top of the cylinder, the lock does not unlock.

A **combination lock** does not use a key. Three **rings** inside the lock turn on one **axis**. (The axis is the straight line around which the rings turn.) The **knob** and **dial** also turn on the axle. Each of the three rings has a **notch** cut into its rim that is shaped like a V or a U.

The dial has a **pin** on its bottom. As the dial is turned clockwise, the pin catches an **arm** on top of the first ring. The dial and the first ring turn together. The first ring has a pin on the bottom and the second ring has an arm on the top. As the dial turns counterclockwise, the first ring turns the second ring. The same action happens between the second and third rings. After three turns of the dial, all three rings are turning at the same time. The rings are turned until each notch is lined up. When all three notches line up, the lock is unlocked.

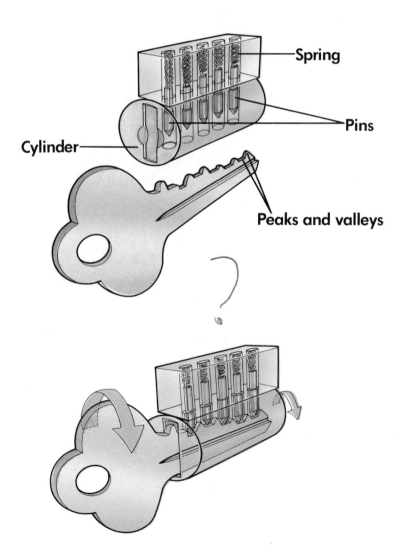

Spring

Pins

Cylinder

Peaks and valleys

Pin-tumbler lock

72

Locks and keys were first used more than 4,000 years ago. They were made of wood and very big. Keys were so long that they were carried on the shoulder.

Combination lock

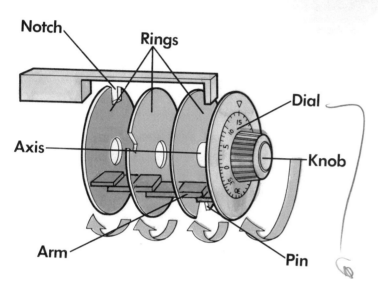

Notch
Rings
Dial
Axis
Knob
Arm
Pin

1. Each lock has its own secret number combination. If the combination is 15-25-35, turn the dial right three times and stop at the number "15." The **third ring** and its notch are set in the correct position.

2. Next, turn the dial to the left. The third ring is free of the pin from the **second ring**. The first and second ring turn together for two turns until the dial stops at the number "25." The notch on the second ring lines up with the notch on the third ring.

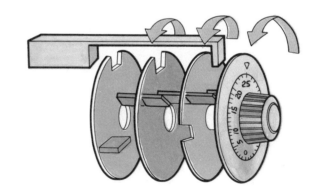

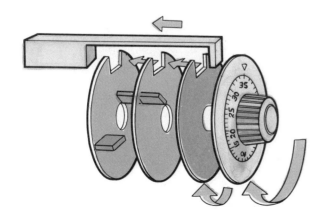

3. Now turn the dial to the right, stopping at the number "35." Only the **first ring** moves. The notch lines up with the other two notches. The lock is open.

Tape recorder and player

How does a tape recorder and player record and play sound?

Most tapes are a strip of plastic coated with a layer of rust. A tape recorder changes sound waves into electrical signals. A tape player changes the signals back into sound waves. Some machines can both record and play back sound.

Sound enters the machine through the **microphone**. The microphone changes the sound into signals. The signals are electrical. The recorder turns the electrical signals into magnetic signals.

During recording, the tape rubs against the **record head**. The recording head is an *electromagnet*. (An electromagnet is made up of a piece of metal and a coil of wire. A coil is a loop. The wire coil wraps around the metal. When electricity runs through the coiled wire, the metal turns into a magnet.)

The magnetic signals change the pattern of the rust particles on the tape. The pattern of the rust particles matches the pattern of the electrical signals.

During playback, the machine pulls the tape across the **playback head**. The tape's magnetic signals send electricity through a coil of wire inside the head. The changes in the flow of electricity match the changes in the magnetic signals. The amplifier (AM-pluh-fyr) makes the signals louder. The **speaker** changes the signals into sound waves that we can hear.

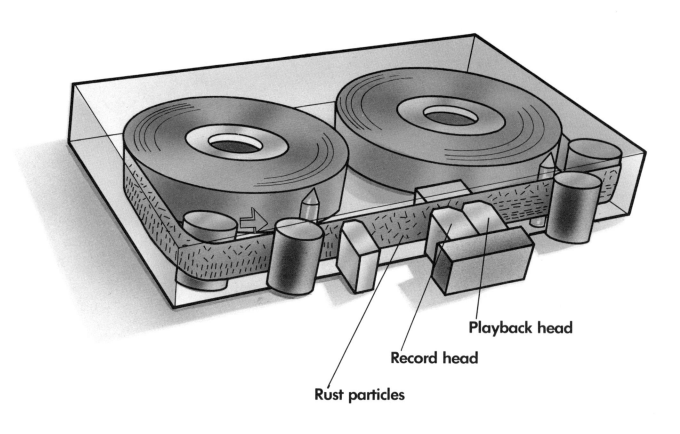

Playback head

Record head

Rust particles

74

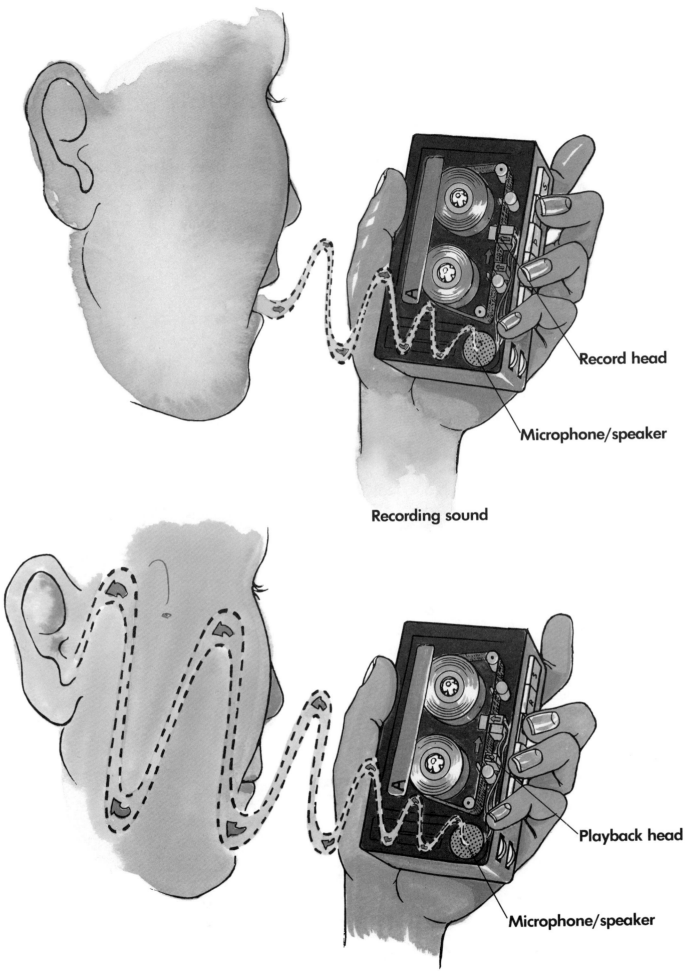

Record head

Microphone/speaker

Recording sound

Playback head

Microphone/speaker

Playing back the recording

Battery

How does a battery carry electricity?

A battery has metals and chemicals inside it that work together to produce electricity. There are two types of batteries—*dry cells* and *wet cells*. Flashlights and toys run on dry cells. Cars and trucks use wet cells.

Electricity is a flow of *electrons*. Electrons are tiny parts of *atoms*. (Atoms are particles that are so tiny they are invisible to the eye. All things are made of atoms.) A flow of electrons makes televisions, washing machines, and many other things work. A battery has two **electrodes** (i-LEK-trodz). One electrode sends out electrons. Another electrode receives, or gets, electrons.

The metal can that is the outside of a dry cell is an electrode. It sends out electrons. Electricity flows out of this electrode. The center post, which is made of the chemical carbon, is another electrode. (The bump on the top of the battery is connected to the post.) It receives the electrons. Electricity flows into this electrode. The space between the post and the tube is filled with a paste. The paste is an **electrolyte** (i-LEK-tro-lyt). The electrolyte makes the electricity flow from the can to the post. The *circuit* (SUR-kuht), or loop, must be a complete circle for electricity to flow.

After a dry cell has been used for a long time, the electrolyte wears out. It cannot conduct electricity. The cell is "dead" and has to be replaced with a new one.

A wet-cell battery works in much the same way. The difference is that it is made of thin metal sheets and a solution of acid. The sheets are made of lead. The acid is the electrolyte. The electricity flows from some lead sheets through the acid to other lead sheets.

Most battery-operated machines, such as a radio, use more than one cell. The cells are loaded with the top of one cell touching the bottom of another. The flow of electricity is stronger than what one battery would produce alone.

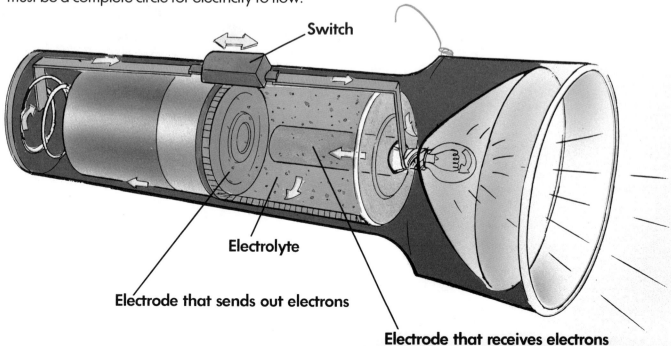

Switch

Electrolyte

Electrode that sends out electrons

Electrode that receives electrons

Toy airplane

How does a toy airplane fly?

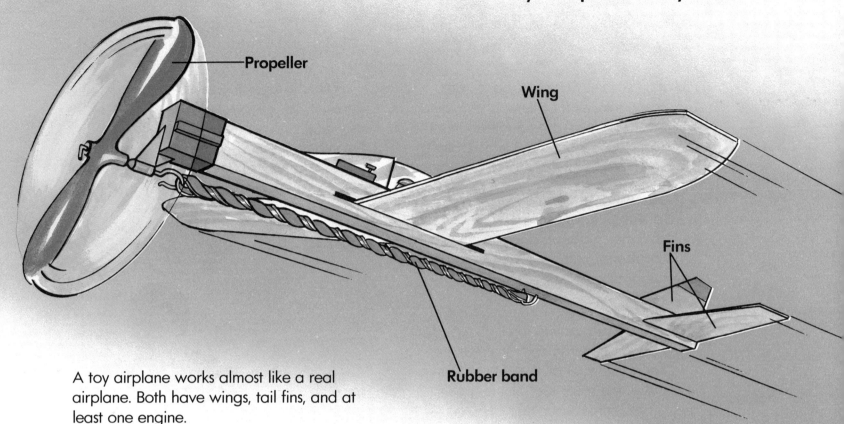

Propeller

Wing

Fins

Rubber band

A toy airplane works almost like a real airplane. Both have wings, tail fins, and at least one engine.

Toy planes are made of a very light wood called balsa (BAHL-suh). After the **wings** have been cut from the balsa, they are bent to curve down at the edges. This wing shape causes *lift* when air passes over and under it. The air moving over the top of the wing must go farther—and faster—to catch up with the air passing under the bottom. This makes the air pressure under the wing greater than the air pressure on top. This difference in pressure "lifts" the wing.

The wings are really made of one piece of wood. The wood piece fits through a slot in the plane's body. The wings are the same length. Slots near the plane's tail hold the **fins**. The fins keep the plane flying straight.

The **propeller** at the nose of the plane hooks to a **rubber band**. The other end of the rubber band is fixed to the plane farther down the plane's body. When the propeller is spun around, the rubber band winds up. The winding rubber band stores energy— just as when a real plane's tank is filled with fuel. Letting go of the propeller makes the rubber band unwind. The unwinding rubber band gives off energy.

Because the rubber band is hooked to the propeller, the propeller spins as the rubber band unwinds. The spinning propeller pushes air backward. This makes the plane go forward.

Television

How do shows get from the television studio to the televisions in our homes?

Television systems have four basic parts. They are a television camera, a transmitter, a receiver (or tuner), and a television set. These four parts work together to bring a scene from a television studio into your home.

A **television camera** takes 30 pictures per second. The pictures are flashed so fast they look as if they make up one moving image. A **microphone** picks up the sound that goes with the pictures.

Prisms (PRIZ-uhmz) inside the camera separate the picture into three images. One image is of all the red color in a scene. Another image is of all the blue color in a scene. And the other is of all the green color in a scene. Each image goes to a **tube.** The tubes change the pictures into electrical signals. These TV signals travel through the air.

The TV station uses a **transmitter** to send the signals to your home. ("Transmit" means "to send.") The transmitter sends the signals through the air in all directions.

Your TV's **antenna** picks up the signals from the air. It sends the signals to the tuner built into the TV set. The tuner *receives*, or gets, the signals. The tuner picks out only the signals for the channel you want to watch. It changes the TV signals into *video* (picture) *signals*. It also separates the *audio* (sound) *signals* from the picture.

The tuner then sends the audio signal to the amplifier (AM-pluh-fyr) and the speaker that are built into the set. The amplifier makes the signal stronger. The speaker turns the signal into sound that you can understand.

From the tuner, the video signal goes to a **decoder**. The decoder picks out the separate red, blue, and green signals that make up the image. It sends these signals to three **electron guns.** (An electron is part of an atom. An atom is a particle that is so small it is invisible to the eye. Everything is made up of atoms.) The electron guns shoot beams of electrons in rows across the picture tube.

The beams hit the back of the **screen.** The inside of the TV screen is coated with **phosphors** (FOS-forz). These phosphors glow when hit by the electron beams, creating the television picture.

In 1924, John Baird was hard at work on something he called a "televisor." It was made up of a tea chest, an empty biscuit box, long needles, an old electric motor, and the lens from a bicycle light. Incredibly, the televisor worked. The distance from the camera to the shadowy picture on the screen was only ten feet, though.

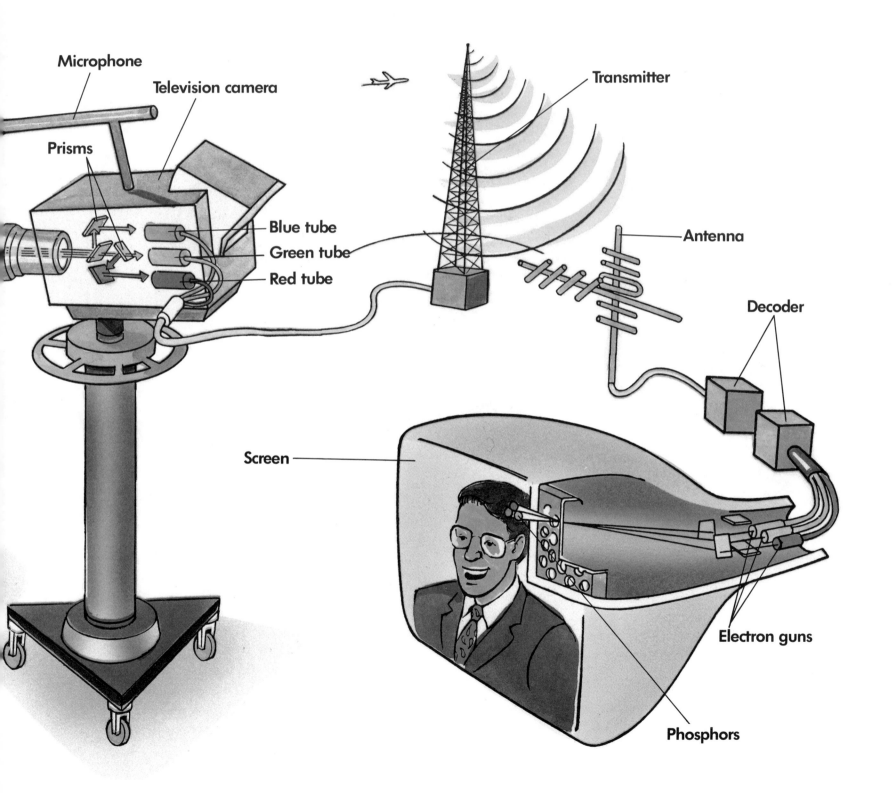

Microphone

Television camera

Prisms

Blue tube

Green tube

Red tube

Transmitter

Antenna

Decoder

Screen

Electron guns

Phosphors

79

Space shuttle

What happens when a space shuttle flies a mission?

To blast into orbit, a space shuttle uses five **rocket engines**. Three rocket engines run on liquid fuel. The other two run on solid fuel. As the shuttle moves toward its orbit, it lets the two solid-fuel rocket boosters fall. Once the shuttle reaches its orbit, it lets go of the large fuel tank for the liquid rockets. The liquid rockets stay on the shuttle.

Rockets in the **tail** of the shuttle steer the ship into orbit. Other rockets in the **nose** and the tail make the ship stay on its path for the whole trip.

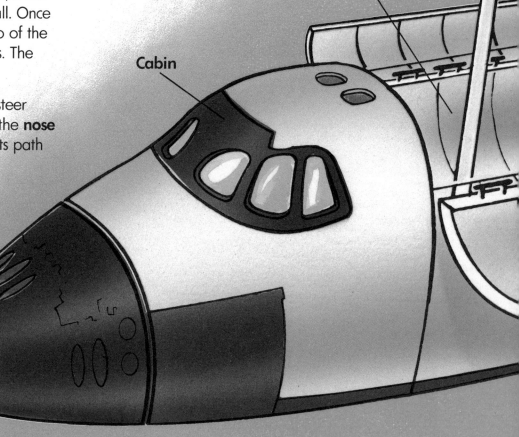

Cargo bay

Cabin

Nose

Each shuttle carries a different **payload**. (A payload is the group of things that are to be carried into space.) Some payloads are top secret. Most have been *satellites*. (A satellite is a man-made object that orbits the Earth, the moon, other planets, and so on.) Satellites have been built to gather information—such as pictures—about our world.

The payload rides in a large **cargo bay** area. The bay opens and a long **robot arm** lifts the load up and out. The arm also pulls loads—such as satellites that need repairs—

into the bay. A crew member works the robot arm from a control panel inside the shuttle. An astronaut works in the cargo area. A **tether** (TETH-ur) **line** keeps the astronaut from floating into space.

The shuttle **cabin** has two sections. The upper section is the flight deck. This is where the mission commander and the pilot ride. The lower section is where the crew sleeps and works. (The shuttle can carry seven astronauts.) It also has a kitchen where the crew members prepare their food.

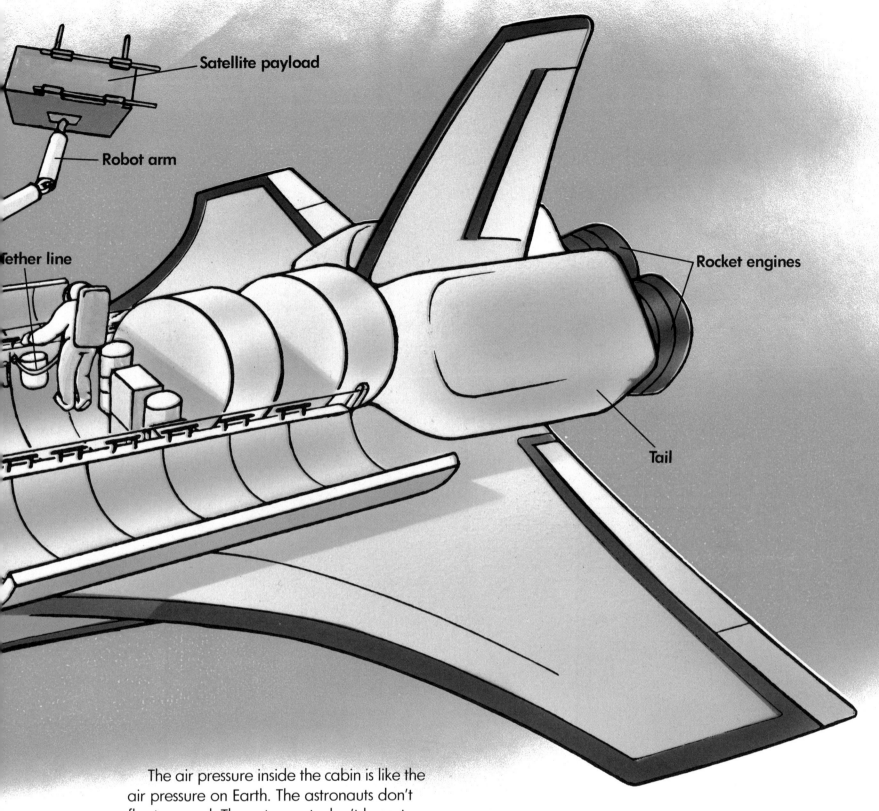

Satellite payload

Robot arm

Tether line

Rocket engines

Tail

The air pressure inside the cabin is like the air pressure on Earth. The astronauts don't float around. The astronauts don't have to wear space suits while working, eating, and sleeping in the cabin. Only when leaving the shuttle do they have to wear space suits.

Rockets in the nose and tail of the shuttle steer the ship out of its orbit when the mission is over. The shuttle comes back to Earth at a speed of almost 16,000 miles per hour. It slows to about 200 miles per hour before gliding to a stop.

The space shuttle launched on April 8, 1984, carried more than 3,000 honeybees. Scientists wanted to know if the honeycombs that bees built in space were the same as the honeycombs they built on Earth. Although the honeycombs were different at first, the bees soon were building honeycombs that were no different from those made on Earth.

Shuttle launcher

How is a shuttle
launched into space?

Fuel tank

Rocket engines

Orbiter

Main engines

USA

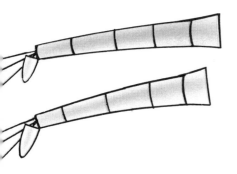

A shuttle launcher is what a space shuttle "lifts off" from. The launcher is made up of four parts. The parts are the **orbiter** (the shuttle), **two rocket engines**, and a large **fuel tank**.

One rocket engine is attached to each side of the large fuel tank. These rocket engines are solid-fuel engines. They are filled with fuel.

The large fuel tank is made up of two tanks. One tank holds liquid *hydrogen*. Hydrogen is the fuel. The other tank holds liquid *oxygen* (LOX). The fuel needs oxygen to burn. There is not enough oxygen in space for the fuel to burn fast enough to keep the shuttle going. The launcher carries its own supply of oxygen. Together, hydrogen and LOX are the fuel for the orbiter's **three main engines**.

Just before the launch countdown reaches zero, the fuel and the oxygen from the large tank are pumped into the shuttle's three main engines. Four seconds later, the two solid-fuel rockets are lit. With all five engines roaring, the shuttle lifts off into space!

The two solid-fuel rockets burn out in a few minutes. As they burn out, they are pushed off and away from the large tank. Parachutes on each rocket open, and the rockets float gently back to Earth. They can be refilled and used again.

After eight minutes, the large fuel tank runs dry and leaves the shuttle. The tank breaks up and falls into the ocean. It cannot be used again.

3-D movie

How can a movie look three-dimensional?

Movies that are three-dimensional (duh-MENCH-uh-nuhl) have images that seem to jump off the screen. Monsters look like they are grabbing at you. Boulders seem to roll toward you. The movie comes to life!

People see in three dimensions. The dimensions are height, width, and depth. Images that have only height and width look flat. Depth makes images look three-dimensional.

We *perceive* (pur-SEEVE), or see, depth because we have two eyes. Our eyes do not see exactly the same thing. Each eye sees an image from a different angle. You can try it yourself. Cover your left eye and look at something. Then cover your right eye and look at the same thing. See the difference? The brain puts the two pictures together. You see one three-dimensional image.

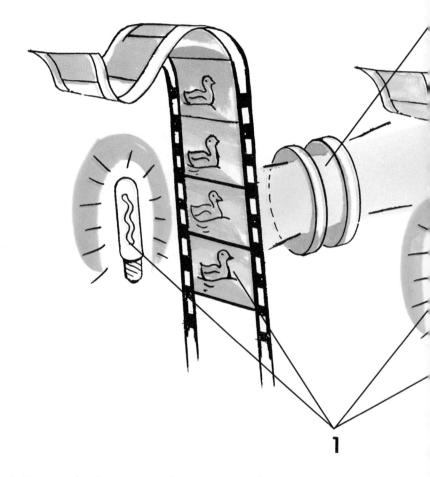

1

1. The film runs through two projectors placed side by side. The two images—each looking a little different—are *projected*, or shown, at the same time.

2. The projectors have **lenses** and **polarizing** (PO-luh-ryz-ing) **filters**. The lenses *focus*, or make clear, the images.

   The two images pass through the polarizing filters. Thousands of tiny lines are cut into the filters. These lines let in the light that each image gives off. One filter has vertical lines. They run up and down. The other filter has horizontal lines. They run across. The filters make the light from the images run in different directions. The images are polarized.

3. The **two images** are projected onto a screen so that they are 2½ inches apart (the distance between our two eyes).

4. To see the image on the screen in three dimensions, the audience has to wear 3-D glasses. The **lenses** of the glasses have the same polarizing filters as the projector. The filter of one lens matches the filter of the projector for the left image. The filter of the other lens matches the filter of the projector for the right image. Each lens only lets in the light from the filter it matches.

   One eye sees one image through the left lens. The other eye sees a little different image through the right lens. Your brain puts the two images together. The picture looks like real life!

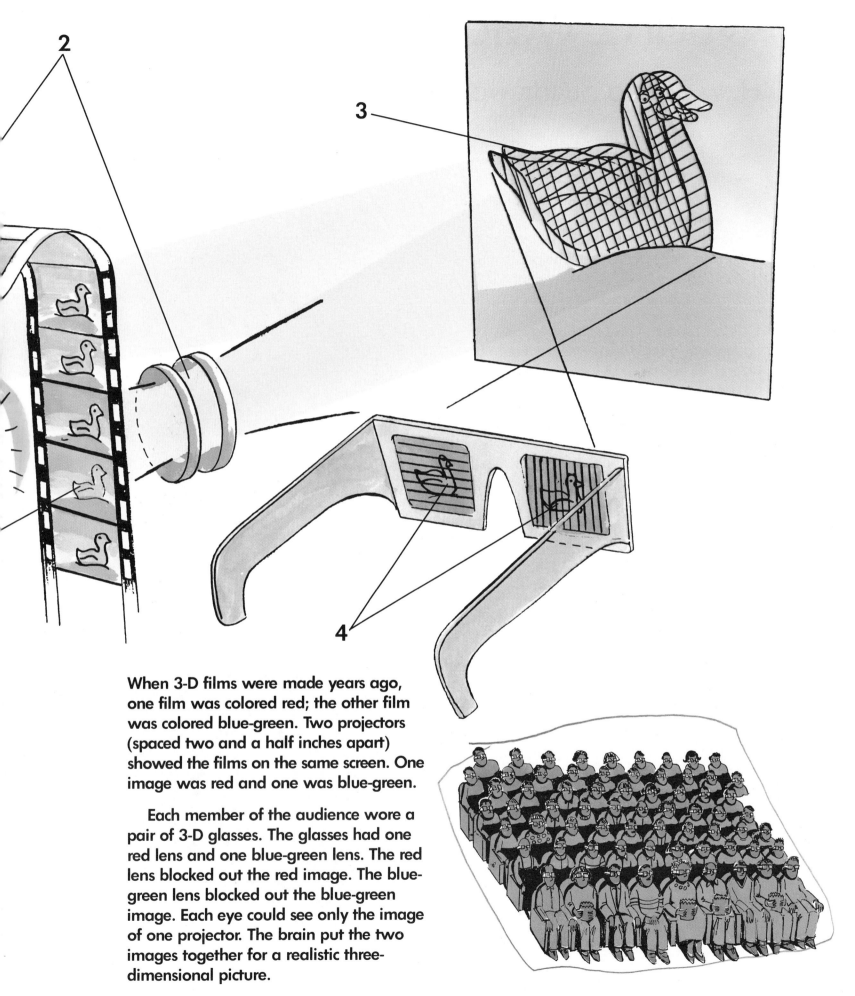

When 3-D films were made years ago, one film was colored red; the other film was colored blue-green. Two projectors (spaced two and a half inches apart) showed the films on the same screen. One image was red and one was blue-green.

Each member of the audience wore a pair of 3-D glasses. The glasses had one red lens and one blue-green lens. The red lens blocked out the red image. The blue-green lens blocked out the blue-green image. Each eye could see only the image of one projector. The brain put the two images together for a realistic three-dimensional picture.

Quartz watch

How does a quartz watch keep time?

A quartz watch uses three basic parts to keep time. The **battery** *stores*, or holds, the energy. The **quartz crystal** *releases*, or gives off, the energy. The energy is released as a group of *pulses*. (A pulse is a beat.) The **microchip** counts the pulses. The pulses must be made at an even rate—they must all beat at the same speed.

A quartz watch uses little energy. (A battery may last for years.) It never has to be wound. It keeps time as long as the battery has energy.

The quartz crystal is a part of the watch's *electrical circuit* (SUR-kuht). (A circuit is a loop.) Electricity flows in a circuit from the battery through the crystal. The flow of electricity makes the crystal *vibrate*—it moves back and forth. The crystal vibrates at a regular rate—32,768 times a second in quartz watches!

A microchip counts the back and forth movements. The microchip sends the signal to different places in different kinds of quartz watches. If the watch has a **liquid crystal display** (LCD), the signal goes to the LCD. The signal tells the LCD to add one second for every 32,768 pulses. If the watch has hands like a clock, the signal goes to a motor. The signal tells the motor to turn a set of gears every 32,768 pulses. (A gear is a wheel with teeth.) The gears then turn the second, minute, and hour hands.

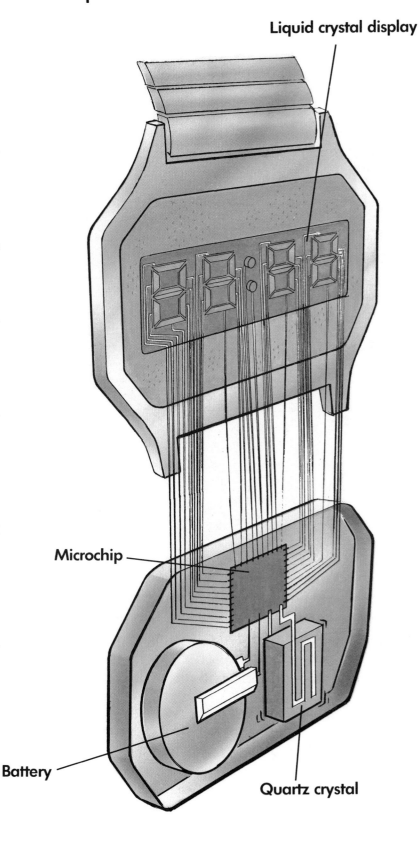

Liquid crystal display

Microchip

Battery

Quartz crystal

Magic slate

How does a magic slate make words and lines disappear?

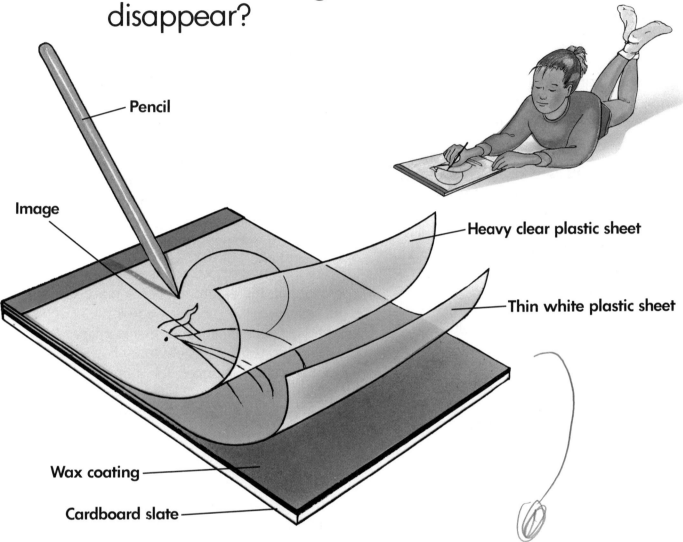

Pencil

Image

Heavy clear plastic sheet

Thin white plastic sheet

Wax coating

Cardboard slate

A "magic" slate is made of cardboard, wax, and plastic. When you write on it, dark lines appear. When you lift the two sheets of plastic, the lines disappear.

The **cardboard slate** is coated with black **wax**. The wax is sticky. Although the **thin plastic sheet** in the middle looks gray, it is really almost white. It is so thin, the black wax can almost be seen through it. This sheet is *delicate* (DEL-i-kuht), too—it tears easily. The **top sheet of plastic** is heavier than the sheet in the middle. It is clear. The marks made on the top sheet will be clear,

too. The top sheet can be plain or it can have puzzles, mazes, and games on it.

The "magic" **pencil** has no lead—only a pointed tip. When the pencil presses against the slate, the thin plastic sheet in the middle sticks to the black wax. The sheet sticks to the wax only where the pencil pressed it against the slate.

Now you see the blackness—and the **image**—clearly. The sticky wax holds the plastic until the two sheets of plastic are lifted. The two sheets of plastic are lifted and the image is gone!

Scrap yard crane

How can a scrap yard crane pick up such big piles of metal?

A scrap yard crane can lift big piles of metal because of a powerful magnet. The magnet can lift several thousand pounds of metal at a time!

The magnet gets its magnetic power from electricity. This kind of magnet is an **electromagnet**. (An electromagnet is made up of metal and wires. The piece of metal is in the center—it is the core. The wires wind around the metal core.)

The flow of electricity through the wire and around the core gives the magnet power. An electromagnet is not a magnet unless electricity flows through it. If a lot flows around the core, the magnet is strong. If a little flows around the core, the magnet is not as strong. If the wire wraps around the core once, the power is weak. If the wire wraps around the core many times, the power is strong. The core is the center point of the magnetic energy.

A scrap yard crane looks like a building crane. The operator sits in a **cab** and works the controls. The crane has controls for the electromagnet and for the **cables**. (The cables are the thick wire ropes the electromagnet hangs from.) The cables run around **pulleys**. (Pulleys are wheels with grooves. A cable rides in the groove.) Behind the cab is a motor and **winch.** The motor turns the winch. The winch raises and lowers the magnet by winding and unwinding the cable.

To pick up a scrapped car, the crane operator puts the electromagnet in place. It is put right over the car. The magnet is lowered onto the metal. The operator flips a switch. The switch sends electricity flowing through the electromagnet. The magnet pulls the scrap metal up. The operator pulls a lever that switches on the winch. The winch lifts the magnet and the scrap into the air.

To drop the scrapped car, the magnet and scrap are put in place. They are put right over the spot the car is to be dropped. The operator switches off the electricity. The magnet drops the scrap metal.

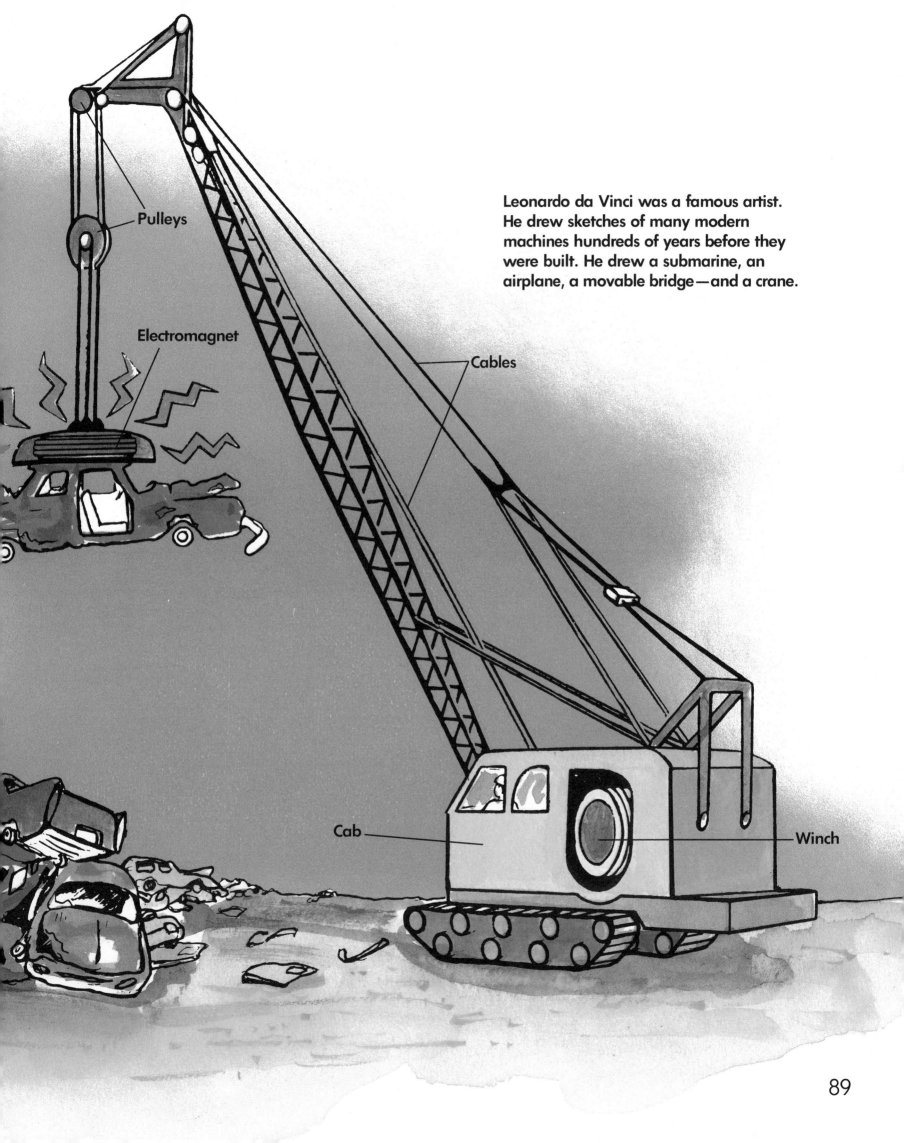

Pulleys

Electromagnet

Cables

Leonardo da Vinci was a famous artist. He drew sketches of many modern machines hundreds of years before they were built. He drew a submarine, an airplane, a movable bridge—and a crane.

Cab

Winch

89

Frisbee flying disk

Why does a Frisbee flying disk fly?

The Frisbee flying disk is named after the Frisbie Pie Company. The Frisbie Pie Company is a bakery that opened in Connecticut more than 100 years ago. For fun, people tossed around the empty pie tins. The tins had the name "Frisbie" printed on the bottom. About 40 years ago, Walter Morrison created metal tossing toys he called "Flyin' Saucers." He later changed the metal to plastic. He also changed the name to "Frisbee."

Anything flat will fly for a short distance—as long as it is thrown so that it spins. The spinning makes the object act like a *gyroscope* (JY-ro-skop). A gyroscope will keep spinning in the same direction until *gravity* and *friction* stop it. This is gyroscopic (jy-ro-SKAHP-ik) force. (Gravity is the force that pulls us to the Earth. Without gravity, we would float. Friction is created when two things rub against each other. Friction slows moving objects down.)

To throw a Frisbee flying disk, you send it forward with a spin. Gyroscopic force keeps it pointing in the same direction you threw it. Throw a Frisbee straight and it flies straight. Throw it at an angle and it keeps flying at the same angle—as long as it has speed. Gyroscopic force will keep the Frisbee spinning at this angle until gravity and friction make it fall. A Frisbee, though, flies farther than does a flat, round disk.

Its shape lifts the Frisbee up into the air. The top is curved and the bottom is hollow. The air passing over the top is spread out over the larger, curved area. The pressure of the air passing over the top is less than the pressure of the air passing under the bottom.

The difference in pressure pushes the Frisbee up. This is *lift*. When the Frisbee starts out, its lift is strong. As the Frisbee slows down, its lift gets weak.

Toaster

How does a toaster heat and brown bread?

Put a slice of bread into a toaster slot and it drops onto a **carrier**. The carrier is the rack that holds the bread in place while it toasts. A lever on the side of the toaster moves the carrier. Pushing down on the lever lowers the bread into the toaster. Pushing down on the lever also flips a switch. The switch turns on the **heating elements** inside the toaster.

The heating elements are made of wire. Electricity passes through the wire, heating it up to 1500°F. The wires are so hot, they glow. A toaster with two bread slots has three heating elements. There is one on each side and one in the middle. These elements heat both sides of the two bread slices at once.

A **thermostat** (THUR-muh-stat) tells when the toast is done. The thermostat is a switch that works at a certain temperature. Set the thermostat to switch off at a low temperature, and the bread is lightly toasted. Set it to go off at a high temperature, and the bread is darkly toasted.

When the temperature inside the toaster is high enough, it triggers the thermostat. The thermostat makes the electricity flow into a **latch**. The latch opens to let go of the carrier. As the carrier moves up, the heating elements turn off. The toast pops through the slots.

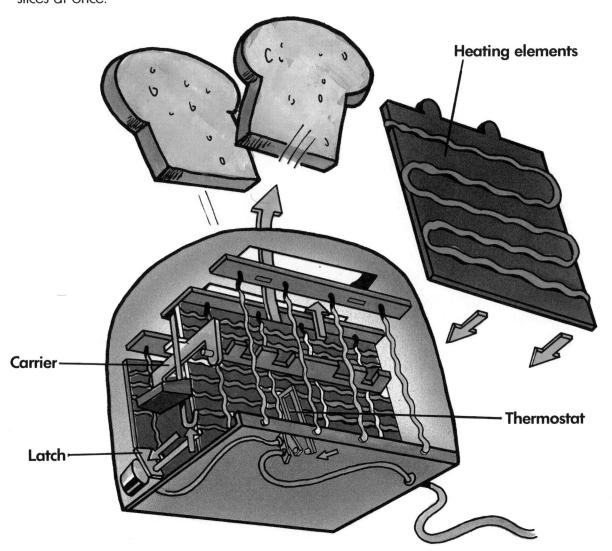

Heating elements

Carrier

Thermostat

Latch

Bumper car

How do bumper cars drive across the floor?

Electricity, not gasoline, makes bumper cars go. Electricity travels in a *circuit* (SUR-kuht). (A circuit is a loop.) The circuit that electricity flows through in a bumper car has three parts. The parts are the **ceiling**, the **tall pole** on the car, and the **floor**.

A **metal net** hangs from the ceiling. The car's pole touches the net all the time. The car's **metal wheels** touch the floor all the time, too. Electricity flows from the ceiling and through the pole. From the pole, electricity goes through the car's motor and into the wheels. From the wheels, electricity goes into the floor. Then it flows back the same way. The circuit is complete.

Electricity drives the motor that makes the bumper car's wheels turn. Turning the wheels makes the bumper car move across the floor.

Once you are safely seated in a bumper car, the operator starts the ride. The ride operator starts the flow of electricity by flipping a switch. Pressing the **foot pedals** controls how much electricity goes to the car's motor. Pressing hard sends more electricity to the motor. The car speeds up. Pressing softly makes the car go slower.

Bumper cars are built to bump other cars. You can go fast or slow, and you can steer —but you can't back up! A bumper car has wheels that turn all the way to the side. Turning the wheels to the side lets you "spin out" of a crash.

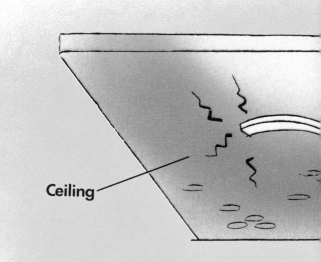

Ceiling

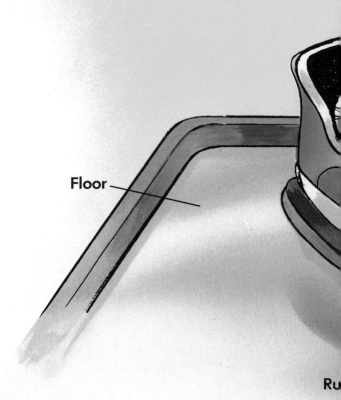

Floor

Ru

Pads inside the car and on the steering wheel keep you from getting hurt. Some cars have shoulder straps. The straps keep you from moving forward in a crash. The outside edge of a bumper car has **rubber bumpers**. They make the bumps less rough.

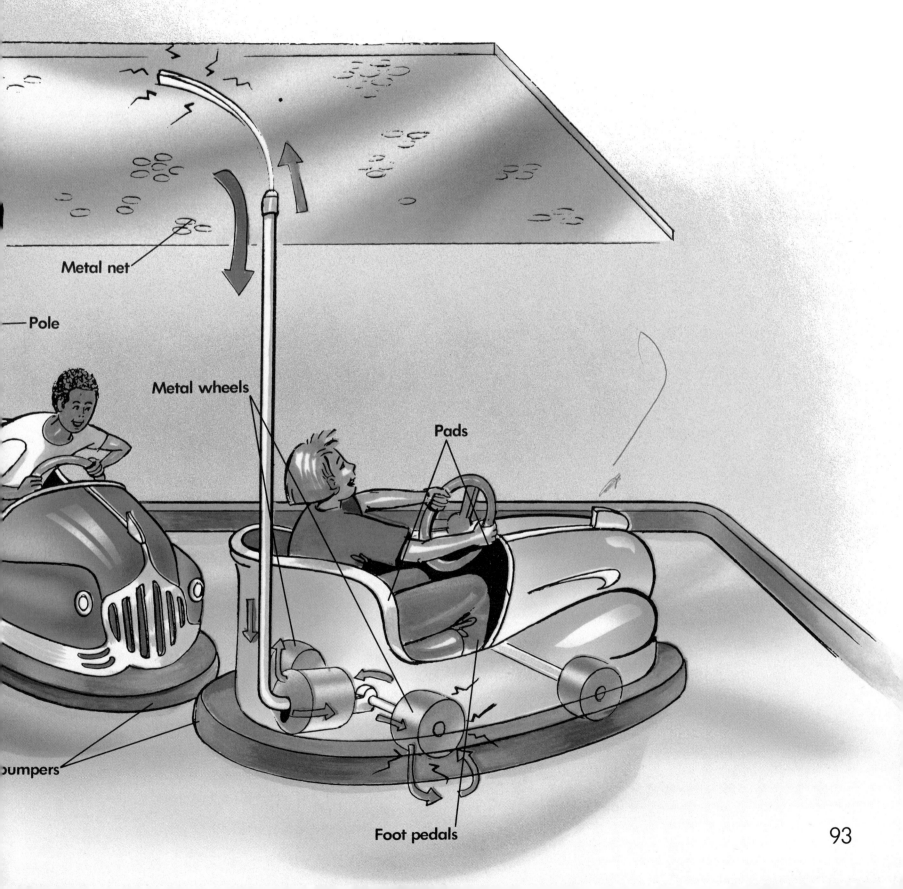

Metal net

Pole

Metal wheels

Pads

umpers

Foot pedals

Escalator

What makes the steps of an escalator go up and down?

Lift the steps out of an escalator and you'll see what look like two huge bicycle **chains** and **sprockets**. (A sprocket is a wheel with teeth.) The sprockets pull the chains. **Step axles** attach the steps of an escalator to the chains. (An axle is a metal rod.) Four small **rollers** on each step run in two smooth tracks. The bottom rollers run in one metal track. The top rollers run in another metal track. The two tracks are close to each other at the middle of the escalator's rise. They are farther apart at the top and bottom of the escalator. The difference in height makes the steps flatten out at the top and bottom of the rise.

A motor turns the sprocket at the top of the escalator. Because the motor can run forward or backward, the escalator runs in either direction. A belt attached to the motor turns the **drive sprocket**. The drive sprocket pulls the chain. The moving steps are all connected to the chain. As they run in a loop around the two sprockets, they carry riders up or down.

The "up" escalator steps start out even. The steps slip from under the **combplate** (KOM-playt). Each step then begins to rise. The two wheels on the front of each step ride the **track** on the **inside**. The two wheels on the back of each step ride the **track** on

the **outside**. Because the inside track is below the outside track, the steps flatten out at the top of the escalator. The steps slip under the combplate at the top of the escalator.

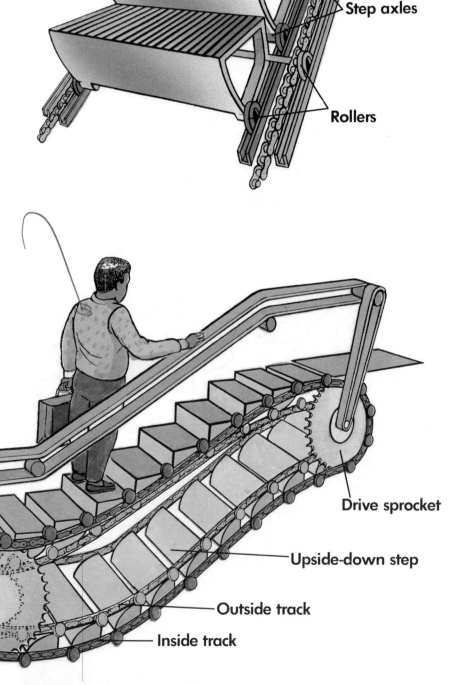

Step axles

Rollers

Drive sprocket

Upside-down step

Outside track

Inside track

Chains

Combplate

Rollers

Sprocket

94

Tops

What makes a spinning top fall?

All tops must spin on their point so as not to fall down. A top acts like a *gyroscope* (JY-ro-skop). A gyroscope will keep spinning at the same speed and in the same direction until *gravity* or *friction* stop it. (Gravity is the force that pulls us to the Earth. Without gravity, we would float. Friction, created when two objects rub against each other, slows moving objects down.)

A top spins until gravity and friction make it fall. Friction is made at the point where the top touches the ground. As friction slows its spinning speed, the top leans. It wobbles. It makes bigger—and slower—circles. At last, the top falls down.

Some toy tops are made to spin with a pull of a tightly wound **string**. Other toy tops are made to spin by pumping a **handle**.

In a pump-handle top, the handle sticks out from the center of the top. A groove cuts into the handle. The groove makes a spiral along the length of the **rod**. A **metal plate** inside the top fits into the groove. A push down spins the top—the metal plate is trapped inside. A **spring** pops the handle up. The top now spins freely (without anything helping it spin).

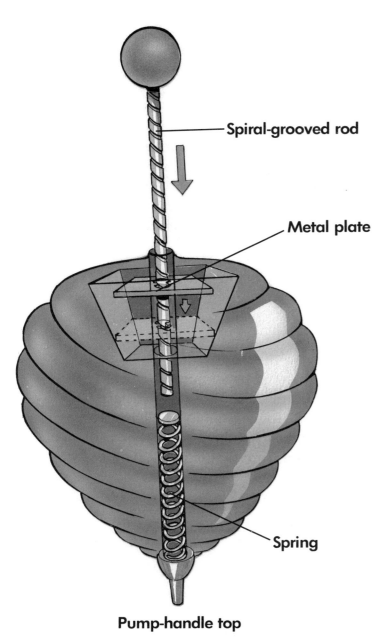

Spiral-grooved rod

Metal plate

Spring

Pump-handle top

Five thousand years ago in Babylonia, a land in the Middle East, children played with tops. The tops were made of clay and were painted with pictures.

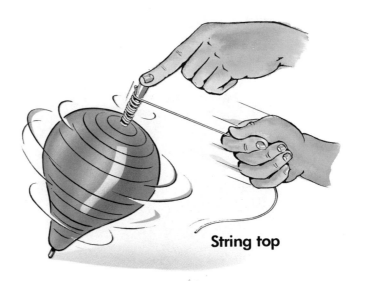

String top

Jet engine

Where does a jet engine get its power?

1. Jet engines (turbojets) have power because every action has an equal and opposite reaction. The *action* is a stream of burning gases bursting out of the back of the engine. The *reaction* is the plane's movement forward.

    To start the action, a large **fan** pulls air through the engine's **front intake**.

2. The air goes into the **compressor**. The compressor is a core surrounded by fanlike blades. The compressor's core is small at the front of the engine and big at the back of the engine.

3. The air flows through sets of **fanlike blades** that *compress* it. The blades "squeeze" the air. Air heats up as it is compressed.

4. The hot air goes into a **combustion chamber**. "Fuel" comes into the combustion chamber through **nozzles**.

The hot compressed air mixes with fuel deep in the combustion chamber. The fuel catches fire and burns.

5. The burning fuel gives off very hot gases. The hot gases shoot past the **turbine blades**. The movement of gases makes the turbine turn. As the turbine turns, it turns the compressor. The compressor blades compress more air, and the action goes on and on.

6. The gases shoot out the **back of the engine**. This action causes an equal and opposite reaction. The plane is pushed forward.

Airplanes powered by jet engines travel at 450 to 500 miles per hour. The fastest jets can reach "Mach (mahk) 3." Flying at Mach 3 is flying at three times the speed of sound. That is nearly 2,000 miles per hour!

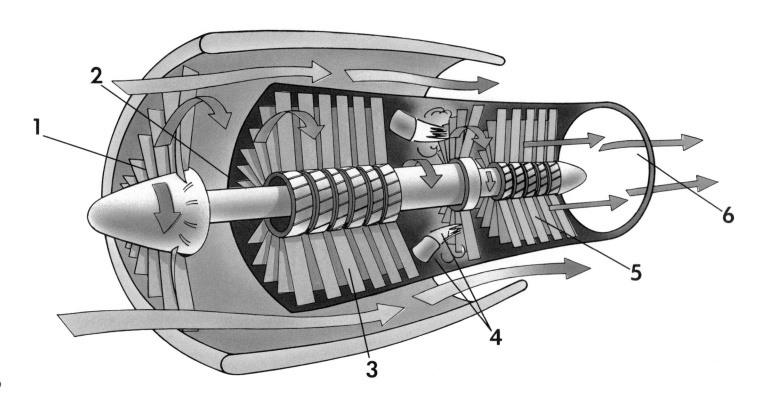

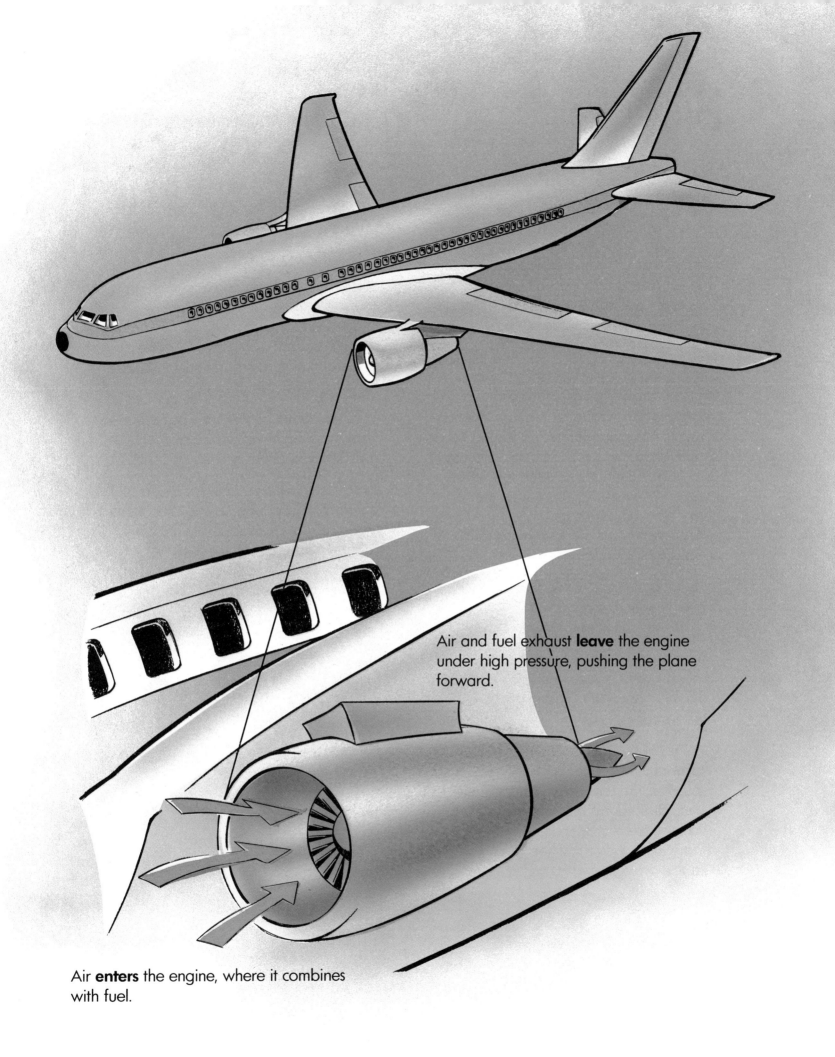

Air and fuel exhaust **leave** the engine under high pressure, pushing the plane forward.

Air **enters** the engine, where it combines with fuel.

Bicycle

How does a bicycle travel?

Bicycles have gone through many changes over the past 100 years. Bicycles of the 1800s had their pedals attached to the front wheel. Pushing the pedals turned the front wheel. Every time the pedal made a whole circle, the front wheel turned around once.

Today's bicycles have pedals that are not attached to the front *or* the rear wheel. The pedals are attached to the front sprocket. (A sprocket is a wheel with pointy teeth.) The sprocket is connected to the back wheel by a chain drive. Turning the pedals turns the sprocket. When the sprocket turns, it pulls the chain. This makes the back wheel turn. As the back wheel turns, it moves the bicycle forward.

1. Pedaling turns the **front sprocket,** which pulls the chain around.

2. The **chain** runs around the front and rear sprockets. This chain is made of round rods linked together. The spaces between the rods match the spacing of the teeth of the sprockets.

3. The chain pulls across the top of the **rear sprocket.** This pulling turns the rear sprocket. The rear sprocket turns in the same direction as the front sprocket. Because the rear sprocket connects to the rear wheel, the rear wheel turns. The bicycle moves forward.

4. Your legs work best pedaling at 60 to 120 revolutions—complete circles—per minute. Bikes come in many "speeds," though. There are three-speeds, ten-speeds, even 21-speeds. Different speeds have rear sprockets of different sizes. A smaller sprocket makes the rear wheel turn faster. Pedaling is harder, though.

A ten-speed bike lets the rider choose between **two front sprockets**. The sprockets are different sizes.

5. To shift sprockets, or gears, the rider pulls on the shift lever. This lever pulls a cable. (A cable is a rope made of wire.) The cable pulls the **derailleur** (dee-RAY-lur or dee-RAY-yur). The derailleur pulls the chain onto the gear that has been chosen.

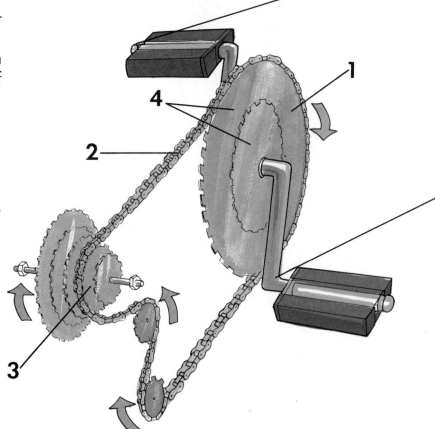

6. Every turn of a sprocket with 40 teeth pulls 40 links of chain.

The **rear sprocket** might have only 40 teeth. As 80 links of chain pass over the rear sprocket, it turns twice. One turn of the pedals produces two turns of the rear wheel.

The rear sprocket might have only 20 teeth. Changing gears to this smaller sprocket means the rear wheel turns four times while the pedals turn once.

7. **Levers** on the handlebars operate the bike's brakes. A tug on the levers pulls a **cable**. The cable runs to the brake.

8. The brake is made up of a **caliper** (KAL-uh-pur) and two **rubber shoes**. Calipers open and close like a pair of pliers. The cable pulls the two halves of the caliper together. This pushes the shoes, or rubber pads, against the wheel's rim. The turning wheel slows down.

9. Turning the handlebars turns the **fork**. The fork connects to the front wheel. Turning the fork points the bike in the direction you will ride.

Personal computer

How can a computer do all the things it does?

1. A personal computer (PC) has many parts to it. It has a "brain"—the **central processing unit** (CPU). And it has a "body." The body is made up of the keyboard, the "mouse," the monitor, the disk drives, the printer, and the software. With all its parts working together, the PC uses and stores (or keeps) information.

2. To use the computer, the person needs a way to "talk" with it. The **keyboard** has the keys that send signals to the CPU. The keys on a computer keyboard look like the keys on a typewriter. Pressing a typewriter key prints a letter or number on paper. Pressing a key on a computer keyboard sends signals to the CPU. The CPU can tell which key was pressed. Some keys type letters and numbers. Others give other commands—they tell the computer to do something. The commands can be to erase, add a word, or print.

3. Some computers have a **mouse**. The mouse, like the keyboard, sends its own signals to the computer. Rolling the mouse over a flat surface moves the *cursor* (KUR-sur). The cursor is the blinking line or square on the monitor's screen. It tells you where you are on the screen. Once the cursor is in place, you can do or change actions on the screen by pressing one or more buttons on the mouse. Different computers use the mouse differently.

4. A computer system also needs a way to "talk" back to the user. A video screen *displays*, or shows, words, numbers, and—on some computers—pictures. The screen is a **monitor**. The screen shows you what you've written or drawn.

5. Computers can deal with a huge amount of information. Some of the information is the program that works the computer. Some of the information is the work you have done. Either way, the information is stored so the computer can use it.

   Information is stored in the computer itself or on **floppy disks**. Floppy disks are the square plastic envelopes that slip inside the computer's **disk drives**. (A disk drive holds the information that runs the computer.) The envelopes hold magnetic disks. The disks can be filled with information much the same way a tape cassette holds music. Many computers have two or more drives—two drives for two floppy disks and a built-in hard drive.

   A hard drive does not use a floppy disk. A hard disk is built into the computer to store information.

6. The computer also can print information out on paper if it is connected to a **printer**. The printer changes signals from the CPU into *characters*. Characters are the symbols—letters, numbers, or signs—that appear on the keyboard. Most printers print in a dot pattern. The dots are arranged to look like the characters. A printer can make changes in the size and shapes of the characters.

7. A computer system can be used for writing, drawing, or lots of other things. It can help you figure out a math problem or it can play a game with you. The different programs are **software**.

Zipper

How does a zipper fasten clothes?

The teeth are the most important part of a zipper. Each tooth is a tiny bar of metal or plastic. One end of the tooth is attached to a **strip of fabric.** The other end of the tooth has a bump on top and a hole on the bottom. All the teeth on the strip line up. The teeth have small spaces between them.

Two strips are fastened together at the bottom so that the teeth are staggered (STAG-urd). The staggered teeth make a zigzag pattern. A tooth from one strip of the zipper fits into the space between two teeth on the other strip. As the two strips come together, the bump on one tooth fits into the hole of a facing tooth. One after another, the teeth fit perfectly into the spaces.

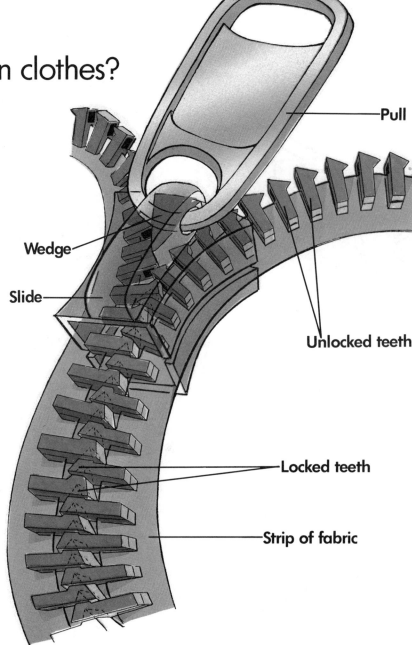

Pull

Wedge

Slide

Unlocked teeth

Locked teeth

Strip of fabric

The **slide** makes the teeth fit together. The slide is Y-shaped inside. It has a **pull**. Tug up on the pull and the slide comes up. As the slide comes up, the two rows of teeth go into the top of the Y—one row on each side. The Y-shape feeds the teeth together at an angle. At the right angle, the teeth lock together. The teeth come out of the bottom of the slide locked together.

Tug down on the pull and the slide goes down. As the slide goes down, the row of locked teeth goes into the bottom of the Y shape. A **wedge** is in the middle of the Y. The wedge forces the teeth to unlock. The teeth come out of the top of the slide unlocked.

X-ray machine

How can an X-ray machine take pictures of bones and muscles in the human body?

X rays are waves. They can travel through some things and not others.

Pictures can be taken with an X-ray machine. The machine uses X rays, not light, to take pictures. X rays are a kind of light energy that the eye cannot see.

X rays come out of a tube. The tube has electricity flowing through it. Particles, or small pieces, from the flowing electricity make a beam. The beam is shot at a piece of metal. When the particles hit the metal,

they give off energy, making X rays. The X rays are powerful. The X rays leave the machine through a **window.**

The X rays travel to the patient. X rays can pass through soft human tissues—like skin—but they cannot pass through bone. The bone absorbs the rays like a sponge absorbs water.

When a leg is put between the X-ray machine and a piece of X-ray film, the rays pass through the soft parts of the leg and go on to the **film**. The bones in the leg absorb the X rays. The film is darker everywhere the rays did not hit it. The film makes a picture of the "**shadow**" of the bone and not the bone itself.

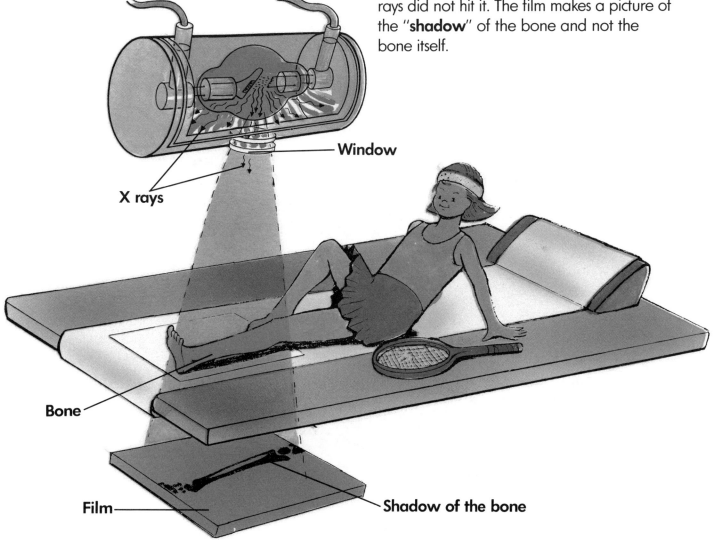

Window

X rays

Bone

Film

Shadow of the bone

103

Kite

How does a kite fly in the sky?

Kites fly because the wind, or air, is strong enough to lift them up and away.

Kites come in many shapes and sizes, from the flat, diamond-shaped kite to the fancy Chinese dragon kite.

The diamond-shaped kite is made of paper or light fabric that is stretched over two crossed sticks. The crossed sticks make a **frame**. The stick that runs the length of the kite is the longer of the two. The place where the two sticks cross is the **point of balance**.

A **string** runs through the edge of the paper and shows through at the four corners of the diamond. The string at the corners fits into **notches**, or cuts, in the ends of the crossed sticks.

Another string is tied to each end of the longer stick. This string is loose and longer than the stick.

A **bridle cord** is tied to the long, loose string. The bridle is the long, long string that wraps around the **winder.** It is easier to hold the winder than to hold a single string. The winder keeps the bridle cord from tangling.

A **tail** is fixed to the bottom of the kite. The tail helps balance the kite as it flies. It keeps the bottom end of the kite pointing down.

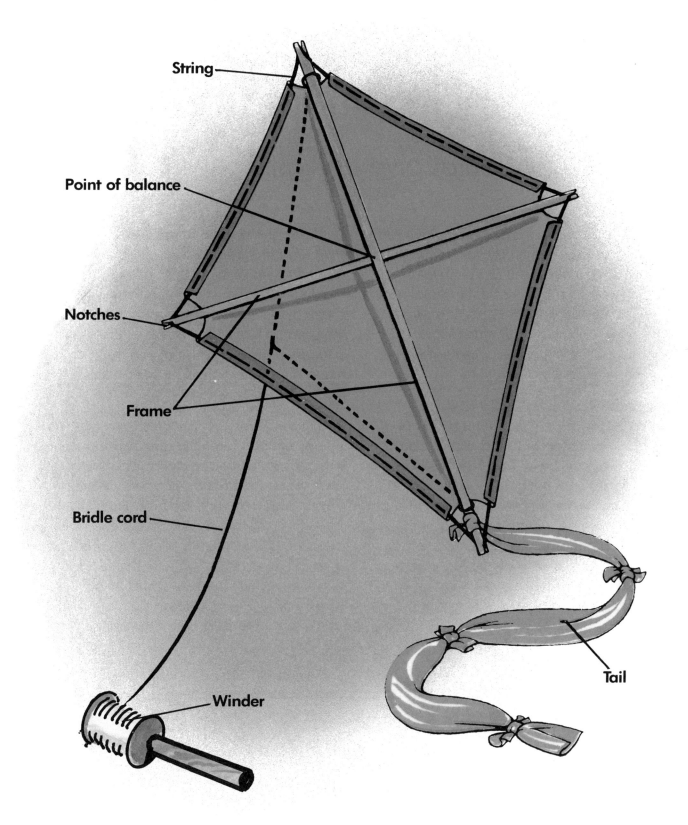

String

Point of balance

Notches

Frame

Bridle cord

Winder

Tail

It is best to run down a treeless hill to put your kite in the air. When you feel a breeze, let out a few yards of string from your winder. Stand with your back to the breeze to watch your kite. You can feel it tugging and needing more string. Let out as much string as you can without letting the kite swoop down. If it begins to drop, rewind some of the string. Once your kite is high in the sky, it will stay there.

The Army and Navy of England used kites during the battles of the early 1900s. The kites could carry people. A train of big box kites was put up in the air. A kite that carried a man was then attached to the train of kites. Once he was in the air, the man could see the enemy.

Lights and switches

How do light bulbs give off light?

A metal glows when it is heated. It glows red first, then yellow, and finally white. The glow is *incandescence* (in-kuhn-DES-uhnts). An incandescent light bulb has a thin metal wire strung in the middle of the bulb. The wire is a filament (FIL-uh-muhnt). Electricity flows through the metal filament. The heated filament glows white.

Lamps use tungsten (TUHNG-stuhn) filament light bulbs. (Tungsten is a kind of metal.) A **tungsten bulb** is a glass globe sealed to a **brass base.** The brass base screws into a light socket. Inside the globe, a glass stem holds up a **wire frame.** The wire frame is two wires that hold up each end of the filament. The **filament** is made of a coil, or loop, of tungsten. Electricity flows through the wire and into the looped tungsten. The tungsten glows with a hot, white light. **Nitrogen**, a gas, fills the bulb.

Streetlights and headlights are halogen (HAL-uh-juhn) light. **Halogen light** is a powerful kind of incandescent light. The **gas** that fills the bulb has a chemical in it. The chemical makes the temperature hotter and the pressure higher in a halogen light than in a tungsten bulb. Because of this, the bulb is made of **quartz** instead of glass. (Quartz does not break as easily.)

The long tubes of light used in schools are fluorescent (flur-ES-uhnt) light. A **fluorescent tube** has **plugs** and **metal rings** at both ends. It does not have a filament. **Mercury vapor,** a gas, is inside the tube. Electricity flows through the vapor and between the metal rings at both ends of the tube. The gas gives off an invisible light when electricity flows through it. The light shines on a **phosphor** (FOS-for) **coating** on the inside of the tube. The tube then glows brightly.

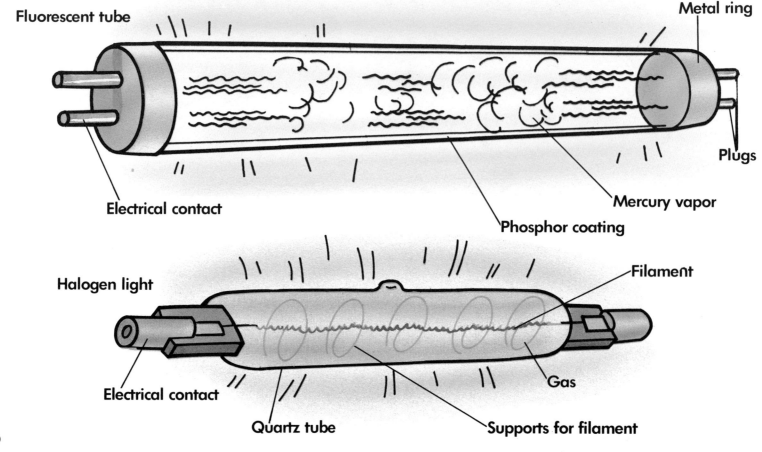

Fluorescent tube

Metal ring

Electrical contact

Plugs

Mercury vapor

Phosphor coating

Halogen light

Filament

Electrical contact

Gas

Quartz tube

Supports for filament

A light switch connects and disconnects wires. It does this by opening and closing contacts inside the switch. Contacts are made where two wires touch. Closing a contact lets electricity flow through. Opening a contact stops electricity from flowing through. Switching on a light connects the bulb to the electricity.

Switches open and close their contacts quickly to prevent sparks. Most do this by using a spring that snaps from open to closed when you flip the **switch lever.**

Toggle switches use a **spring.** The spring snaps the switch from open to closed. A **yoke** is the metal piece that connects the contacts. When the switch is in the "on" position, the yoke touches both **contacts.** Electricity flows to the light. Switched to "off," the yoke does not touch both contacts. Electricity does not flow to the light.

Electricity was first used in the White House, the home of the president, in 1891. Benjamin Harrison was the president of the United States then. Afraid of the lights, he would not touch the switches. Many times, he slept with all the lights on.

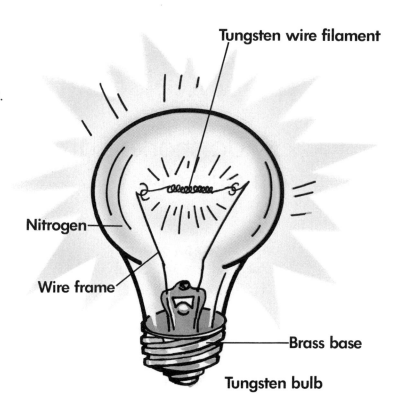

Tungsten wire filament

Nitrogen

Wire frame

Brass base

Tungsten bulb

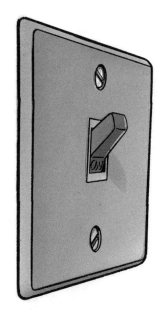

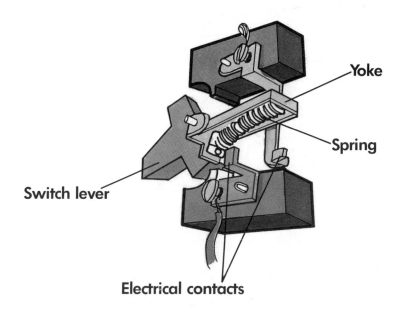

Yoke

Spring

Switch lever

Electrical contacts

Off

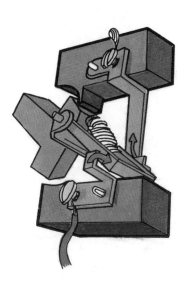

On

107

Snorkel and scuba gear

How do snorkels and scuba gear help people swim and dive?

A **snorkel** is used for swimming just below the water's surface. A snorkel is a hollow tube with a mouthpiece at one end. The top of the tube stays above the water. By keeping the mouthpiece in his or her mouth, the swimmer can breathe while swimming.

The **mask** that covers the eyes and nose helps the swimmer in two ways. The mask protects the eyes without blocking what a swimmer sees. The mask also keeps water from going up the swimmer's nose.

For deeper swimming, the diver uses a *Self-Contained Underwater Breathing Apparatus—scuba*, for short. Scuba gear is made up of a **tank** and a **regulator** (REG-yuh-layt-ur).

Tank

Mouthpiece

Hose

Regulator

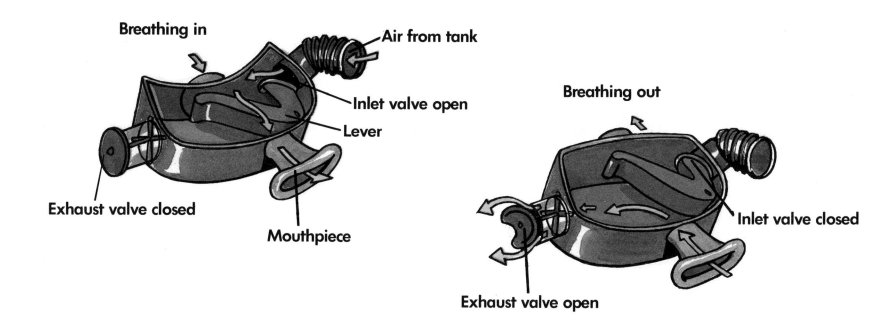

Breathing in

Air from tank

Inlet valve open

Lever

Exhaust valve closed

Mouthpiece

Breathing out

Inlet valve closed

Exhaust valve open

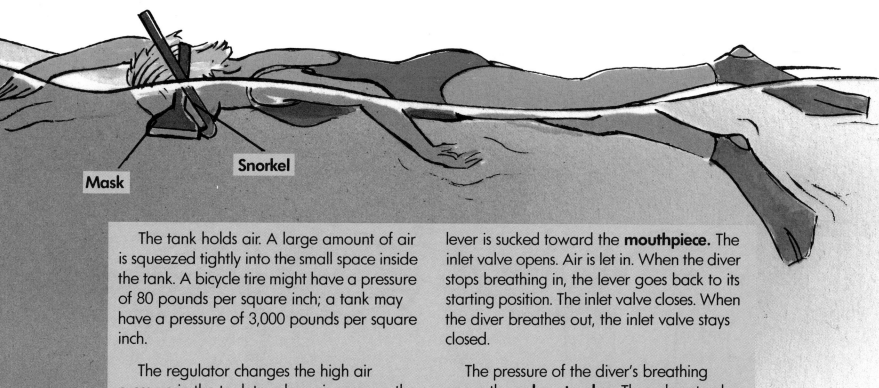

Mask

Snorkel

The tank holds air. A large amount of air is squeezed tightly into the small space inside the tank. A bicycle tire might have a pressure of 80 pounds per square inch; a tank may have a pressure of 3,000 pounds per square inch.

The regulator changes the high air pressure in the tank to a low air pressure the diver can breathe. The lower-pressure air flows from the tank through a **hose** to the **inlet valve.** A **lever** opens and closes the inlet valve. When the diver breathes in, the

lever is sucked toward the **mouthpiece.** The inlet valve opens. Air is let in. When the diver stops breathing in, the lever goes back to its starting position. The inlet valve closes. When the diver breathes out, the inlet valve stays closed.

The pressure of the diver's breathing opens the **exhaust valve.** The exhaust valve lets the used air out into the water. This is the stream of bubbles you see above and behind a scuba diver.

109

Robot

How can a robot do the work of people?

Robots are all around us, and most don't look human at all.

A robot is really a computer with an attachment—such as an "arm"—that lets it work.

One type of robot is simply a metal "arm," "wrist," and "hand." The robot can reach, grab, and turn to do a job. For instance, a robot arm can be made to tighten **bolts** in car engines. (A bolt is a rod that has a head on one end and a spiral on the other.) The hand may be a **wrench** that fits onto the bolts. The **arm** reaches out until the wrench fits onto each bolt. The wrist turns to tighten each bolt.

Valves make the arm, wrist, and hand work, and a computer controls the valves. (Valves are short tubes through which gas or liquid flows.) The valves let oil flow through different parts of the arm, wrist, or hand. The flowing oil makes the parts move.

The valves are controlled by the computer. The computer uses a feedback system to move the valves. The computer, for example, tells the arm where to move. A signal tells the computer when the arm has moved there. The computer then sends signals to the arm to go on to the next step.

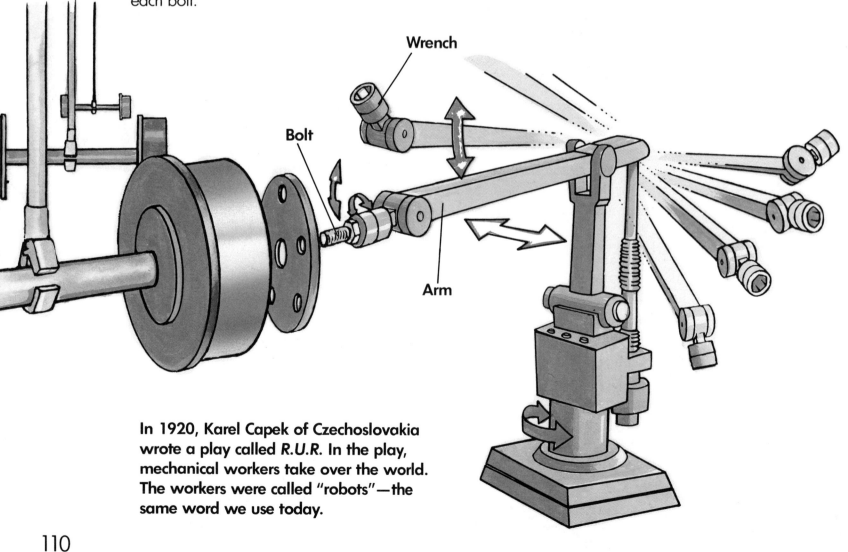

Wrench

Bolt

Arm

In 1920, Karel Capek of Czechoslovakia wrote a play called *R.U.R.* In the play, mechanical workers take over the world. The workers were called "robots"—the same word we use today.

Air bag

How can an air bag protect the driver when there is a crash?

1. An air bag works only if the front end of the car hits something or is hit. It will not work if the car is hit from the side or from behind. The air bag pops out only in a crash that happens at 12 miles per hour or more. Even at 12 miles per hour—not very fast for a car—the driver can be hurt.

An air bag works *automatically* (aht-uh-MAT-ik-lee)—it works on its own. The driver does nothing to make it work.

2. An air bag is like a big balloon. The cloth bag is kept in the center of the steering wheel. The crash sends a signal to the air bag. The air bag *inflates* (in-FLAYTS), or blows up, faster than the blink of an eye. The air bag is filled with gas in less than a second (the gas is harmless).

3. The air bag protects the driver in a crash. Instead of the driver hitting his or her head against a hard steering wheel, the driver hits a soft air bag.

4. If the air bag stayed inflated, the driver could not see over the bag to steer to the side. An air bag *deflates* (dee-FLAYTS), or flattens, in another blink of the eye. The gas escapes through the cloth bag.

Microwave oven

How does a microwave oven cook food so fast?

Other forms of cooking—a flame, hot air—cook food from the outside in. A microwave oven makes the food heat itself. It cooks food from the inside out.

Microwaves pass through glass, paper, and most plastics. They bounce off metals. And they are *absorbed*, or soaked up, by water and fats. Many foods are mostly made of water and fats.

The water and fats in food are made up of molecules (MAHL-i-kyoolz). (Molecules are tiny particles that are invisible to the eye.) The molecules that make up water and fats are *charged* by electricity. One end of each molecule has a positive charge. The positive charges are shown here by "+" signs. The other end of each molecule has a negative charge. The negative charges are shown here by "-" signs.

The opposite ends *attract*, or pull toward, each other. Positive charges pull toward negative charges. Negative charges pull toward positive charges. This is how these molecules line up.

When a microwave hits a molecule, the molecule tries to turn so that its charge lines up with the charge of the microwave.

As the microwaves bounce around inside the oven, they change direction millions of times per second. This makes the food molecules turn around just as fast. The turning makes *friction*. (Friction is made when two things rub against each other.) Friction makes heat—enough heat to cook the food.

Water and fats are made up of molecules.

The molecules line up their charges with the microwaves.

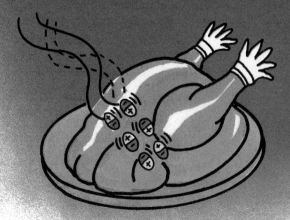

The movement of the molecules makes friction, and friction makes heat.

112

1. The microwaves are made by a **magnetron** (MAG-nuh-trahn). A magnetron is an electrical magnet.

2. The microwaves go into the oven through a **wave guide.**

3. A **fan with metal blades** stirs the microwaves and sends them bouncing around the oven. If the microwaves are not spread out evenly, parts of the food will be burnt and parts will be raw. Stirring the waves cooks the food evenly.

4. The **walls** of microwave ovens are metal. When the microwaves hit the walls, they bounce right off.

5. The **microwaves** that bounce onto the food are absorbed by the water and fats in the food.

6. A metal screen in the **glass door** protects the cook from the waves. Microwave ovens are built so they cannot be used with the door open.

The first microwave ovens were invented more than 40 years ago. They were almost as big and heavy as refrigerators. In 1952, the first microwave oven for the home was made. It cost about four times what a microwave oven costs today.

113

Video games

How can video games be played on a television screen?

Most video game systems are made of a **base unit, game cartridges,** and **controls** (like a joystick).

The base unit holds a small computer. The computer uses microchips to work. One computer chip is the brain of the system. The brain chip is the microprocessor (MY-kro-PRAH-ses-or).

Game cartridges plug into the base unit. Each game cartridge has its own computer chips. These chips hold the computer programs that make up the game. The programs are the instructions for the game. The metal strips at the end of each cartridge are **connectors.** They connect the chips inside the cartridge to the microprocessor inside the game system. The game cartridge also has information about sound and pictures.

The video game controls hold many switches. These switches are often buttons and levers. One control makes the characters move around the screen. It is really four switches in one. Each time you push down on the right side of the switch, it sends a pulse into the system. The pulse is a signal. The pulse tells the microprocessor to move the character to the right. The same thing happens when you press the up, down, and left buttons. And when you press the buttons to fire a missile or start over, it sends these pulses to the microprocessor, too.

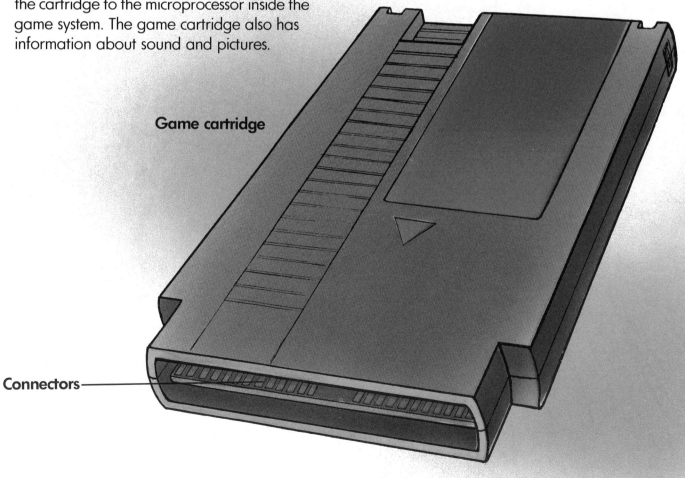

Game cartridge

Connectors

The microprocessor changes the commands you give with the joystick into the sounds and pictures you see on the TV screen. Once the microprocessor understands the commands, it sends commands to two other chips in the base unit. One chip is the pictures chip. The pictures chip makes the characters look like they are moving. The other chip is the sound chip. The sound chip makes music and sound effects.

One of the newest types of games seems more like using a computer than playing a game. These games are *interactive games*. You have to do more thinking to play interactive games than other video games.

Base unit

Controls

In interactive games, you explore lands, castles, or caves. As you play, you have to tell the computer what you want it to do. Do you want it to look around, dig, or jump over a pit? If you don't do the right thing, you might miss finding the treasure or you might fall off a cliff.

Mirrors

How do different kinds of mirrors reflect images?

A mirror is a sheet of glass. It has a thin, silvery coating on the back. Light waves travel through the glass and bounce off the silver coating. The mirror *reflects* the image.

When you are looking straight into a mirror, your image is exactly the opposite of you. Light waves hit the mirror in one direction. They bounce off the mirror at the same angle and in the opposite direction. The image looks *reversed*. You have seen it yourself many times. You have waved your right hand in the mirror. The image in the mirror has waved its left hand back at you.

A **two-way mirror** lets people on one side see through it—like a window—while people on the other side see only a mirror. Two-way mirrors have a thinner silver coating than a regular mirror has. In front of the mirror is a brightly lighted room. (The front of the mirror is the side without the coating.) Behind the mirror is a room that is darker. The person behind the mirror can see through the back of the mirror. The people in front of the mirror see only their reflections.

Two-way mirror

Long ago in China, people placed mirrors near the roofs of their houses. The Chinese people believed the mirrors would reflect away evil things.

Mirrors

How do different kinds of mirrors reflect images?

The glass of a **concave mirror** curves up at the edges. The curve makes an image look bigger than the object. You see a smaller area than if the mirror were flat, though.

The glass of a **convex mirror** curves down at the edges. This curve makes an image look smaller than the object. You see a bigger area than if the mirror were flat, though.

In a **flat mirror**—the kind in your bedroom or bathroom—the reflection is the same size as the object. The reflected image looks as if it comes from behind the mirror. Remember: The image looks reversed.

Convex mirror

Flat mirror

Concave mirror

Temperature-sensitive toy

Why does a temperature-sensitive toy change colors?

Some toys change color in water and some change color in sunlight. Some even change color while you hold or play with them. They are all *temperature-sensitive* toys. They change color as they get hotter or colder.

Toys that change color are made with a special chemical. The chemical changes as the temperature changes. Dyes are added to the chemical. The dye is what gives the toy its colors. The dye changes color when the chemical changes temperature. The chemical may be in the paint finish on a toy car. It may be in the fabric of a doll's bathing suit. It may even be in the toy's plastic.

A temperature-sensitive toy that is dipped in water can turn many colors. Dipping a blue plastic submarine in cold water might turn it green. Dipping it in warm water might turn it purple. And dipping it in hot water might turn it dark green-blue.

The change in color happens every time the toy is dipped in water. As the toy dries it turns back to its original color.

Airplane

How does an airplane fly?

An airplane's wing—the part that keeps it in flight—is like a bird's wing. Both are curved on top and almost flat on bottom. This shape is an **airfoil** (AYR-foyl). When the airplane moves forward, air flows over the top and bottom of the airfoil. Since the top of the airfoil is curved, the air that flows over it has farther to go than the air that flows under it. The air moving over the top of the airfoil must go faster to catch up with the air passing under the bottom. The faster the air moves, the lower its pressure is. This makes the air pressure under the wing greater than the air pressure on top. This difference in pressure "lifts" the wing—it pushes the airfoil up.

To create the flow of air, the plane must move forward. To move forward, most small planes use one or more propeller engines. The engine of a plane is like the engine of a car. The **propeller** is like the blades of a fan. The propeller engines make the plane fly forward because every *action* has an equal and opposite *reaction*. As the slanted blades turn, they throw air backward. This is the action. As the air flows backward, it pushes the plane forward. This is the reaction.

The pilot steers the plane with two pedals and a steering column. The pedals move the **rudder** (RUHD-ur). (The rudder is a movable fishlike fin on the plane's tail.) When the

Propeller

Aileron

Rudder

Elevator

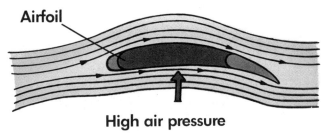

Low air pressure

Airfoil

High air pressure

rudder points straight back, air flows right past it. The plane flies straight ahead. When the rudder moves to one side, it pushes the air to that side. The air pushes the tail, sending the plane in a new direction. When the rudder turns to the right, the plane turns to the right. When it turns to the left, the plane turns left.

To climb, the pilot pulls back on the control column. To drop, the pilot pushes forward on the control column. Moving the control column drives the elevators. (The elevators are the fins that run across the tail.) Just as with the rudder, the elevators steer the plane in the direction they are turned.

The control column also moves the **ailerons** (AY-luh-rahnz). The ailerons are the flaps on the edges of wings. The ailerons move in and out to change the shape of the wings. The pilot uses the ailerons to climb right or left, to roll, and to fly upside down.

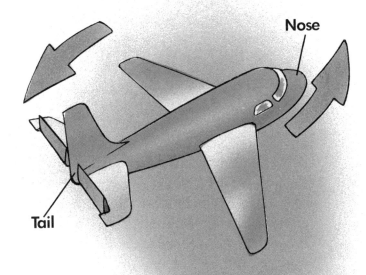

Nose

Tail

Pulling back on the control column tips the elevators up. Tipping the elevators up creates a stream of air that pushes the **tail** down. The **nose** of the plane points up. The plane climbs. Turning the elevators down creates a stream of air that pushes the tail up. The nose of the plane points down. The plane drops.

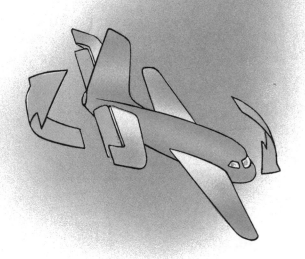

Many others tried to build airplanes before Orville and Wilbur Wright. One try was "The Bird-Powered Flying Machine." The inventor attached several large birds to a balloon. The idea was that they would flap their wings and the balloon would fly away. The birds would not flap their wings, though, and the flying machine stayed on the ground.

Camera and film

How does a camera make pictures out of film?

Cameras make pictures (photographs) on film. Film is a thin sheet of plastic and chemicals. The film's chemicals make an emulsion (ee-MUL-shuhn). As light shines on the emulsion, it changes it. An image, or picture, of the light is made on the film. The camera controls the light that changes the emulsion. The film is then *developed*, or made, into a negative.

The image in a negative is *reversed* from the image in a picture. The dark shades in a black-and-white negative are the light shades in a picture. The light shades in a negative are the dark shades in a picture. A color negative has three layers. One layer changes in red light, another in green light, and another in blue light.

Negatives are used to make prints. The print is the picture itself. Black-and-white film makes **black-and-white prints**. Color film makes **color prints** (and **color slides.** A color slide is a piece of the negative itself. Shining light through the slide *projects*, or shows, an image onto the screen). Shining light through the negative onto special paper makes the print. The dark spots on the negative block the light. Only a little light shines on the paper. With less light, the paper makes a lighter image. The lighter spots on the negative let the light through. A lot of light shines on the paper. With more light, the paper makes a darker image. This process reverses the light and dark areas of the image. The picture is perfect!

Instant cameras make a picture right away. These cameras use **film that develops itself.** As the film is pulled from the camera, the **rollers** spread chemicals that change in light over the film and paper. Light develops the picture right before your eyes.

Color slide

Instant film and rollers

Black-and-white print

Color print

Instant print

1. Looking through the **viewfinder** lets you see what you will be taking a picture of.

2. Light comes into the camera through the **lens.** A camera lens may be several small lenses. These lenses *focus,* or make clear, what the camera "sees." Light from the image must be focused onto the film so that a picture can be made. Some cameras focus themselves.

The shutter blocks the light from the film until you are ready to take the picture. The shutter can be behind, in front of, or in the lens.

3. Pressing the **shutter release** opens and closes the shutter faster than you can see. That is enough time for the light to change the film's emulsion. The longer the shutter is open, the more light shines on the film. The more light the film gets, the lighter the picture will be.

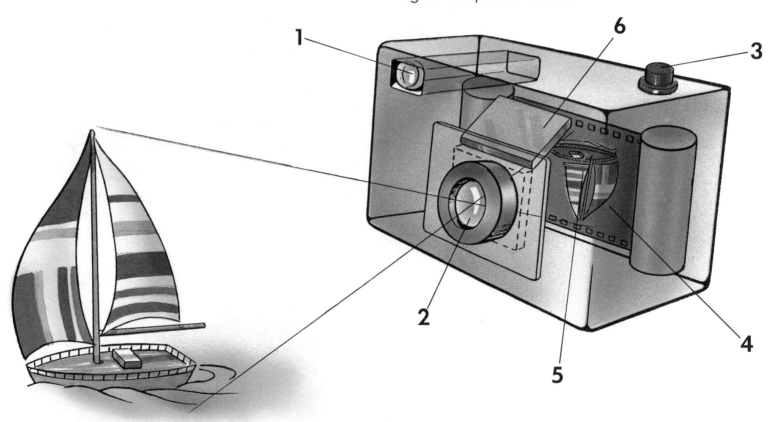

4. The film moves through the camera **frame** by frame. A frame is the film that is needed to take one picture.

5. The light passes through the lens and shines on the film. A camera that has one lens makes an **upside-down image** on the film.

6. A **mirror** reflects the image that is sent to the viewfinder. The image looks right-side up.

George Eastman invented a camera in 1888. He wanted to give the camera— and film—a name that began and ended with the letter "K." It was his favorite letter. It was the first letter of his mother's name. Putting together different letters, he came up with the name "Kodak." Today, Kodak is a giant maker of cameras and films.

Remote-controlled toy

How can a toy be controlled from far away?

Radio waves can carry more than just sound. Remote-controlled toys use radio waves to carry signals from the controls to the toy. These signals make the toy move.

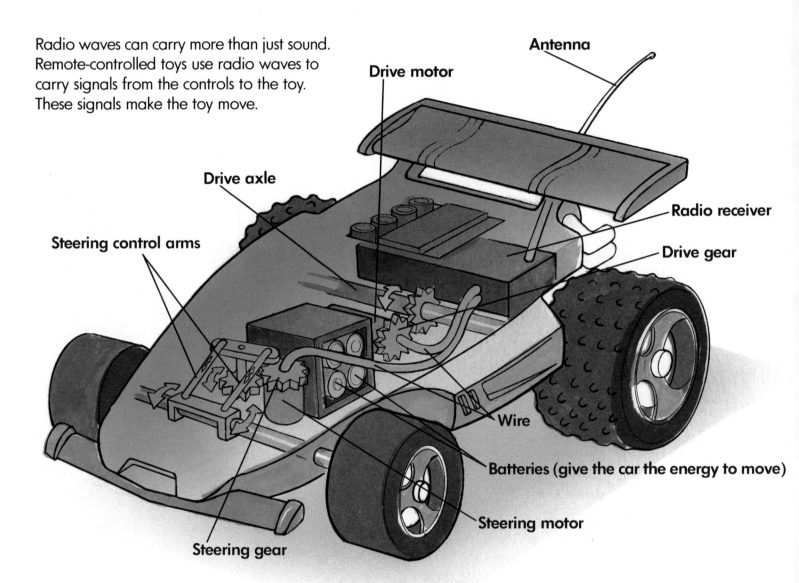

Drive motor

Antenna

Drive axle

Radio receiver

Steering control arms

Drive gear

Wire

Batteries (give the car the energy to move)

Steering motor

Steering gear

Inside the control is a transmitter. The transmitter sends a signal through the control's antenna. ("Transmit" means "to send.") An antenna on the toy picks up the signal and carries it to the toy's receiver. ("Receive" means "to get.") The signal switches the toy's motor on or off. The control and the toy must be close enough for the signals to reach the toy.

A toy car needs more than just a few signals. It can do more than just stop and go. A remote-controlled car can steer, speed up, and slow down.

On a toy car, a motor is used for each type of control. These motors are *reversible*. They can go opposite ways—fast or slow, right or left, backward or forward. The control panel has a **lever** for each motor. (Some controls use buttons, joysticks, or small steering wheels.) The signals for forward and backward movement do not get mixed up with the signals for left and right turns.

The transmitter in the car's control unit sends out signals over its **antenna.** The **antenna** on the car receives the signals. It sends them to the toy's **radio receiver.** The receiver has **wires** that connect to an electric motor. The motor turns gears in the car. (A gear is a wheel with teeth.)

One signal travels through the wire that is attached to the **drive motor.** The drive motor turns the **drive gear.** As the drive gear turns, it turns another gear. This other gear is attached to the **drive axle.** The drive motor makes the car go fast or slow.

Another signal travels through the wire that is attached to the **steering motor.** The steering motor turns the **steering gear**. As the steering gear turns, it turns the gear that is attached to the **steering control arms**. The steering control arms make the car go left or right.

Some control systems are different. Pressing a button, for example, might change the direction of the motor. Letting up on a button and pressing it again might swing the car out of a right turn and into a left turn.

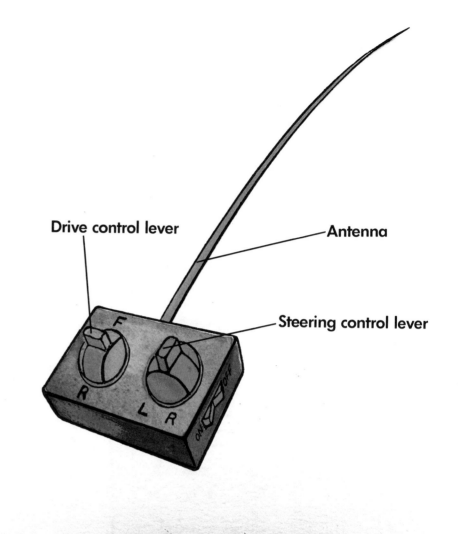

Drive control lever

Antenna

Steering control lever

125

Noisemakers

How do doorbells, car horns, and sirens make sound?

A **doorbell** isn't really a bell. It is a *chime*. A chime makes a sound like a bell makes. The sound is made by a metal **striker** hitting one or more **chime plates.**

Pressing the button of the doorbell closes a switch. Closing the switch lets electricity flow to an **electromagnet**. (An electromagnet is a core, or center, of metal with wire wrapped around it. When electricity flows through the wire, the metal core turns into a magnet.) The electromagnet pulls the striker to one of the chime plates. It makes a musical sound. When the doorbell button is released, the electricity is switched off. The electromagnet stops pulling the striker. A **spring** pushes the striker back into place. The striker hits the other chime plate. Another musical sound is made. The chimes may be tuned differently. One chime may make a high sound. The other may make a low sound.

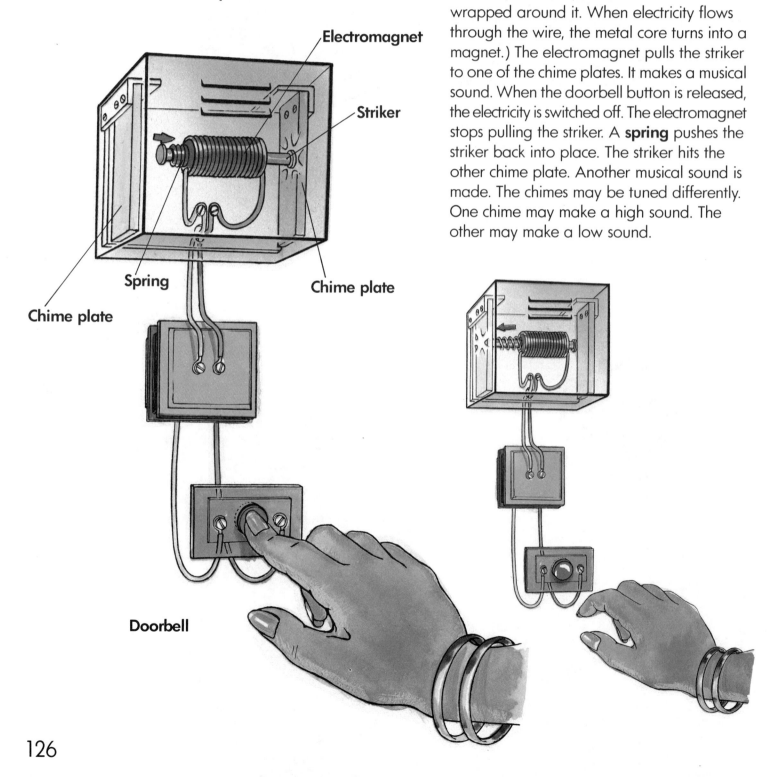

Electromagnet

Striker

Chime plate

Spring

Chime plate

Doorbell

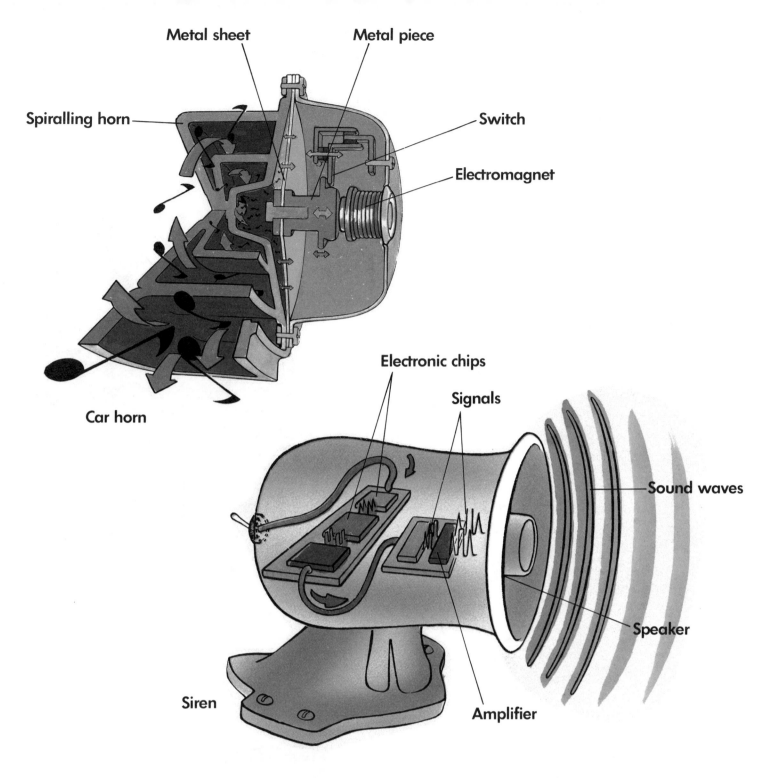

Metal sheet

Metal piece

Spiralling horn

Switch

Electromagnet

Car horn

Electronic chips

Signals

Sound waves

Speaker

Siren

Amplifier

A **car horn** also uses an **electromagnet.** Pressing the middle (usually) of the steering wheel closes a **switch.** Closing the switch lets the electricity flow to the electromagnet. The electromagnet pulls a **metal piece**. The metal piece is fixed to a **thin metal sheet**. As the electromagnet pulls the metal piece, it shuts off the electricity. The metal piece springs back, turning the electricity on. This step is repeated many, many times a second. Repeating this step makes the metal sheet *vibrate*. (To vibrate is to move back and forth.) The metal sheet makes a high sound as it vibrates. The sound travels through the

horn. The horn is shaped like a spiral. The sound is made louder and louder as it travels toward the opening.

Sirens can make many sounds. They can make noises like cries and squeals. They can play the sound from a radio. And they can sound like normal sirens.

Inside the siren, **electronic chips** make signals. The **signals** go to an **amplifier.** The amplifier makes the signals louder. A **speaker** changes the signals into sounds and sends them out into the air for you to hear.

Piano and harp

How do pianos and harps make music?

A **piano** has 88 **keys**. Some are white and some are black. Inside the piano, the keys connect to levers, leather strips, cushions, wires, and hammers.

A metal frame inside the piano holds a row of wires. The wires are stretched on the frame. Under the wires is a piece of wood. The wires are the **strings** of the piano and the wood is the sounding board. It is the sounding board that gives a piano its special sound.

Pressing the **key** drives the **hammer** against the string. The hammer falls back into place right away. A **check** keeps the hammer from bouncing back up to the string and hitting it again. A tiny **spring** underneath raises the key as soon as the key is let go.

Keys

Pedals

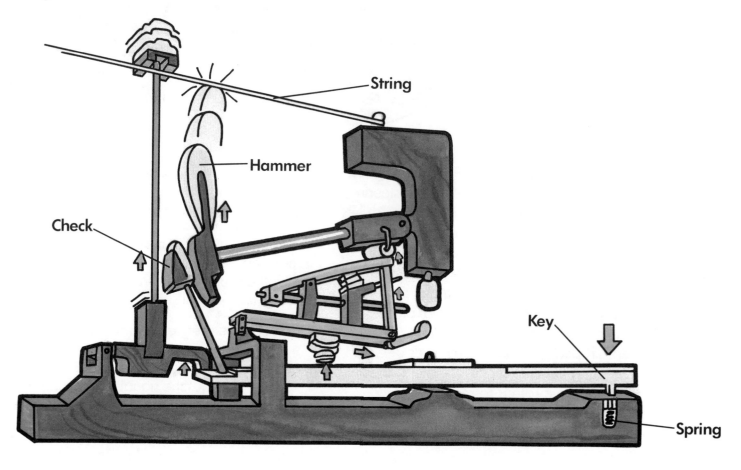

String

Hammer

Check

Key

Spring

When the hammer hits the string or strings above it, a sound is made. The sound is different with each key that is played.

Although a piano has 88 keys on the outside, it has more than 200 strings on the inside. The deep notes are each made by a string wrapped in wire. The middle notes are each made by two strings played at once. The highest notes are each made by three very fine strings played at once. (One of the strings alone would not make a sound loud enough to be heard.)

Lifting the top of a grand piano lets the sound from the sounding board bounce off the top and into the audience. The **pedals** control dampers. Dampers can soften the tone or make it louder and more lasting.

A **harp** has hundreds of **strings**. Each string plays a different note. Plucking the strings with a finger makes the strings *vibrate*. (To vibrate is to move back and forth.) The sound of a string comes from its vibrations.

The strings are stretched on a frame. Each string ends in an empty box. The box is the **sounding board**. The sounding board makes the vibrations of the strings louder and fuller.

The tops of the strings are caught between sets of **pegs**. One set of pegs sits on each **disk**. Pressing a **pedal** turns the disk. As the disk turns, it shortens the length of a string. A short string has a higher sound than a long string.

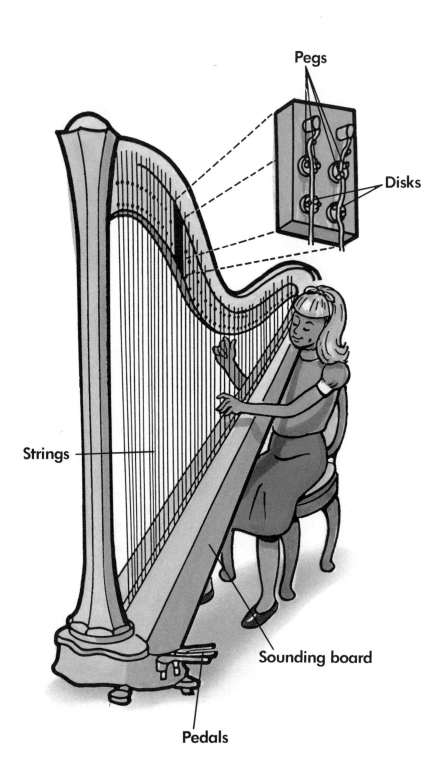

Pegs

Disks

Strings

Sounding board

Pedals

129

Movie makeup

How can movie makeup change actors and actresses into monsters?

1

Many make-believe movie creatures are created with *latex* (LAY-tex). Latex is a creamy liquid that changes to a rubbery "skin." Liquid latex can be poured into a mold of any shape. It can be molded into the shape of a wrinkled forehead, a big nose, or the head of a space alien. Left to set, it gets hard.

When the latex is peeled out of the mold, it is painted and decorated. It is then fitted to the actor.

1. Making an actor into a space alien is easy. A mask is made for the actor to wear.

   A model of the actor's head is made first. The model—not the real head of the actor—is used to make the mask. Next, the head of a space alien is carved in clay over the model of the actor's head.

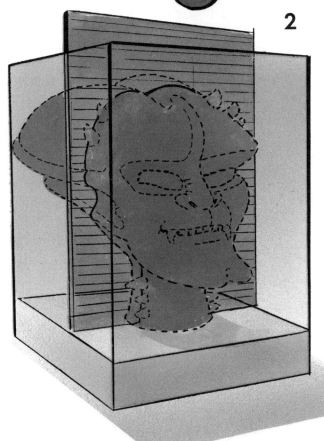

2

2. The model of the space alien's head is placed inside a shell. Plaster is poured into the shell. The plaster flows around the mold, sits, and gets hard. A thin wall sits between the front and back of the shell. The wall lets the two hardened blocks of plaster come apart so that the alien's head can be taken out.

3. There are now two molds *imprinted* with the space alien's head. The molds have the marks of the space alien's head. One mold is of the alien's face. The other mold is of the back of the alien's head. The molds are then placed around the model of the actor's head.

Liquid latex is poured into the mold. It fills the space between the model head and the imprint of the alien's head. The two molds are tightly put together so that no latex leaks out.

4. When the latex has dried and hardened, the two molds are pulled apart. A mask has been made. It is a rubbery latex mold of the model of the alien head. The mask fits like a "skin" on the actor's head. Holes will be cut into the face part of the mask so the wearer will be able to see and breathe. The mask will be painted.

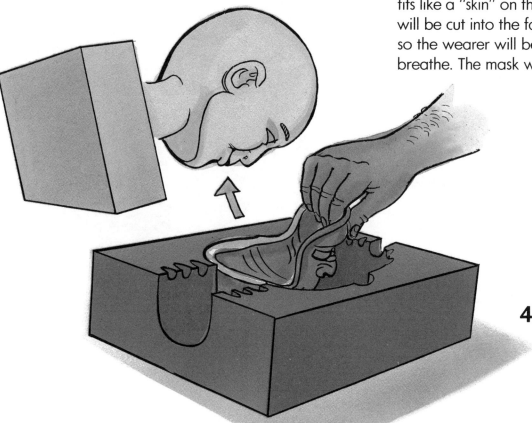

Movie makeup

How can movie makeup make an actor or actress look old?

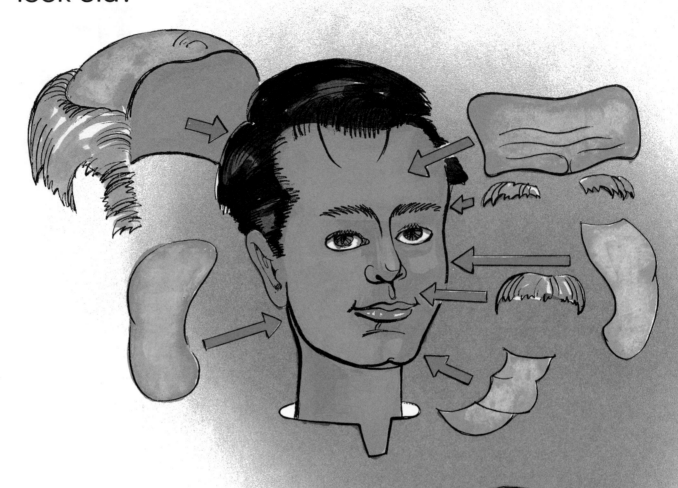

To make a young person look old, patches of latex are molded to look like wrinkled skin. The latex patches are fixed to the actor's face with a special glue. Makeup is put on over the patches and the actor's real skin to blend them together. Topped with a wig or a latex bald head, the actor may have an idea of how he will look when he gets old!

Pitching machine

How does a pitching machine throw a baseball?

Pitching machines—no matter what kind— can throw every kind of pitch.

One type of pitching machine uses two **rubber wheels** and a motor. A motor spins the wheels. The wheels turn in opposite directions. Because they turn in opposite directions, they turn toward and into each other. As they turn into each other, the wheels grip the ball from the **feed tube.** They hold the ball for a second, then fire it out a **chute.**

Pitching machines have **controls.** The controls change the turning speed of the wheels. Changing the speed of the wheels changes the speed of the pitch. A pitching machine can shoot a ball from 40 miles per hour to almost 100 miles per hour.

And each wheel can be set to spin at different speeds. A pitching machine can then throw trick balls—curves, sliders, change-ups, and knuckleballs.

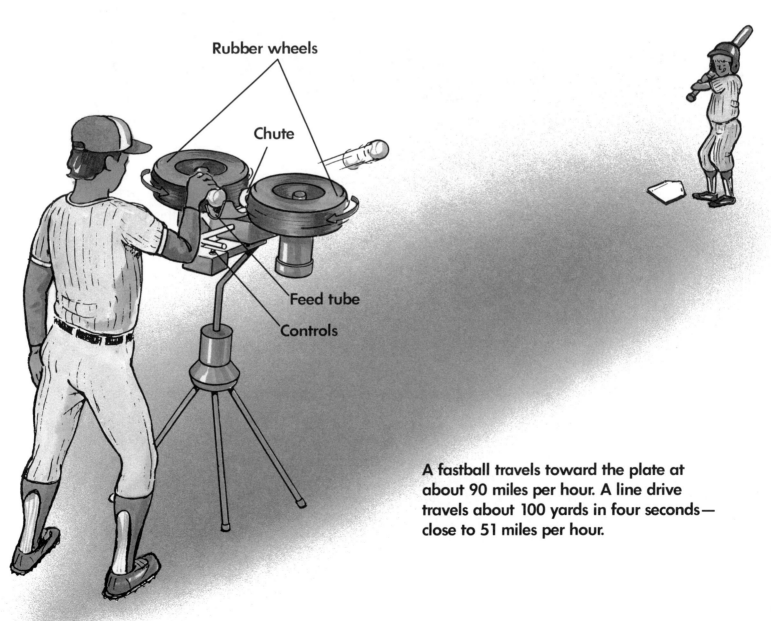

Rubber wheels

Chute

Feed tube

Controls

A fastball travels toward the plate at about 90 miles per hour. A line drive travels about 100 yards in four seconds— close to 51 miles per hour.

Calculator

How does a calculator do arithmetic?

A calculator is like a tiny computer: It can do math problems *automatically* (aht-uh-MAT-i-klee), or on its own.

Inside a calculator is a microchip. (A microchip is very small.) Thousands of parts may be connected on the microchip. These parts are connected in *circuits* (SUR-kuhts). (A circuit is a loop.) When you press the keys of a calculator, you are controlling some of the circuits on the microchip. You are sending signals to the circuits that "do" the math problem—addition, subtraction, and so on.

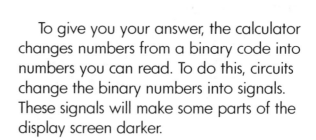

To give you your answer, the calculator changes numbers from a binary code into numbers you can read. To do this, circuits change the binary numbers into signals. These signals will make some parts of the display screen darker.

The screen has seven short lines on it. These seven lines go in different directions. A number can be formed by showing only some of the lines. The number eight is the only number that is made of all the lines.

Because we have ten fingers, people began counting in groups of ten. We call this kind of counting a *decimal* (DES-uh-muhl) *system*. "Deci" comes from the Latin word for "ten." The circuits in a calculator can be only "on" or "off." This system of two choices is a *binary* (BY-nuh-ree) *system*. "Bi" comes from the Latin word for "two." A "1" means the circuit is "on." A "0" means the circuit is "off." Any number can be written as a binary number.

Look at the number five that is shown. When a signal is sent to one of the seven lines, that line is made dark. The rest of the display stays light. Your answer looks like dark "printing" on the screen. The part of the display screen that receives no signal stays light. The part that does receive a signal turns dark. When all the right parts are made dark, you have your answer.

Parachute

How does a parachute stop a skydiver from falling to the ground?

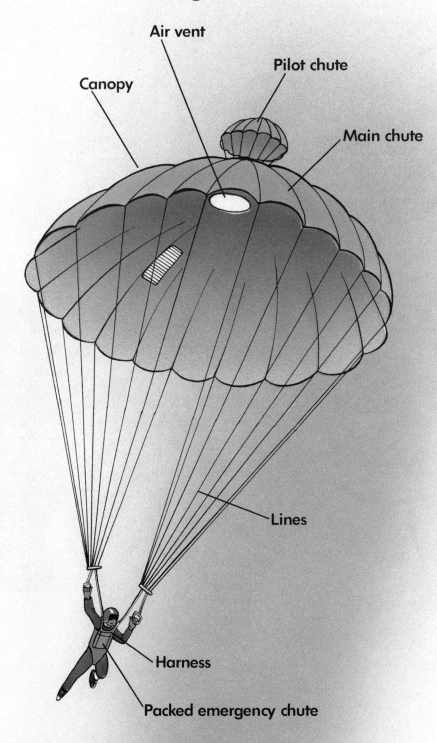

Air vent

Pilot chute

Canopy

Main chute

Lines

Harness

Packed emergency chute

An object falling toward Earth falls very fast unless its *surface area* is made bigger. (Surface area is the size of something when it is laid out flat.) When its surface area is made bigger, the falling object slows down. Friction (FRIK-shuhn)—the rubbing between the air and the object—slows the falling object. A parachute has enough surface area to slow a falling person so he or she can land safely on the ground.

Before leaving the plane, the parachutist folds the chute, fits it into a pack, and carries it on the back. Parachutists carry an **emergency chute**, too. The parachutist wears a **harness**. The harness is made up of straps that go around the body, between the legs, and over the shoulders. The chute's **lines** are attached to the shoulder straps.

After jumping from the plane, the parachutist waits a few seconds before pulling the rip cord. The rip cord is attached to a pin. When the pin is pulled out, the **pilot chute** pops out. When air catches the pilot chute, it pulls the **main parachute** out of the pack.

Once air fills the main chute, the parachutist's fall slows from 150 feet per second to only a few feet per second. A parachute ride could be rocky if there were no **vents** in the **canopy.** (A vent is an air hole.) The **vent** at the very top lets air flow out of the canopy evenly. Because the vent is in the center, air flows through the chute in a straight line. Without the top vent, air would spill out from the sides of the chute. The parachutist would swing dizzily all the way down.

Telephone

How does a telephone make and get phone calls?

1. **Lifting a telephone handset** sends a message to an office of the phone company. The signal travels in a split second. It says you are ready to make a call. The dial tone—the humming sound—signals you to go ahead.

2. A handset has two jobs. In the **mouthpiece,** it changes sound waves into electricity waves. In the **earpiece,** the handset changes the electricity waves back into sound waves.

136

3. Pressing **push buttons** on a phone sends tones (beeps) over the phone **wires.** The tones tell the phone company's computers where your call is going. Pressing "1" tells the computer you are making a call to someone far away. The next three numbers tell what area you are calling. The next three numbers tell the computer what *exchange* you are calling. This connects you with another office. The last four numbers tell the phone company's computer the phone to ring.

6. The signal makes the **called phone** ring. If that phone is being used, you get a busy signal (a fast beeping tone).

When the person you are calling lifts the handset, the ringer shuts off. The connection is completed in less than two seconds!

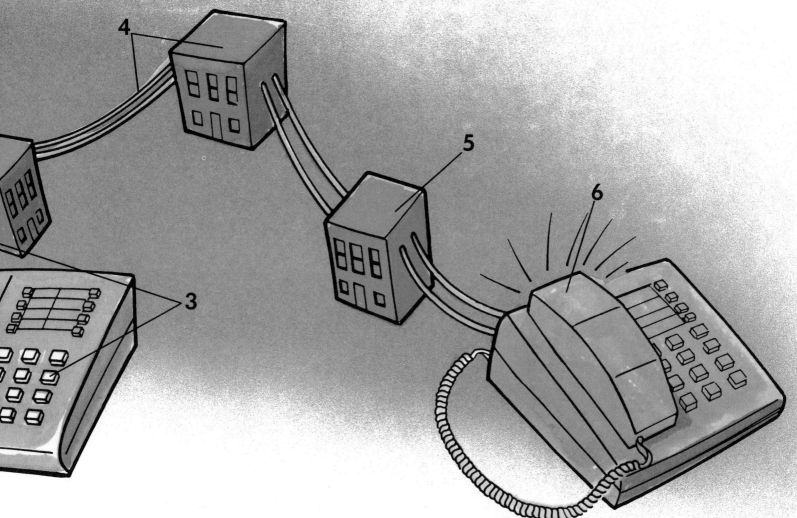

4. The electrical signals flow through the **phone company's system.**

5. When the connection between you and the person is complete, the **exchange** sends a signal to the called phone.

Alexander Graham Bell's mother couldn't hear very well. To help her, he spent much of his life trying to invent a hearing aid. He didn't make a hearing aid, but his work led him to invent the telephone in 1876.

Carousel

How does a carousel make the animals go up and down as it turns around?

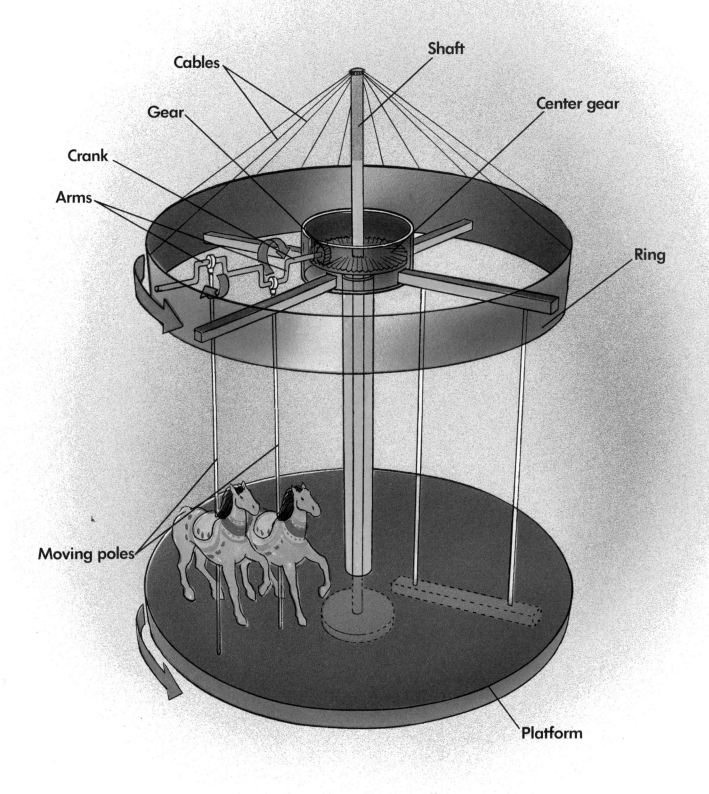

Cables

Shaft

Gear

Center gear

Crank

Arms

Ring

Moving poles

Platform

The carousel probably started out as a tool to train the king's knights in the Middle Ages. A knight-in-training would ride a wooden horse while trying to hit a small target with the tip of his spear. Over the years, the target was changed to the brass ring. Today, catching the brass ring wins the carousel-rider a free ride.

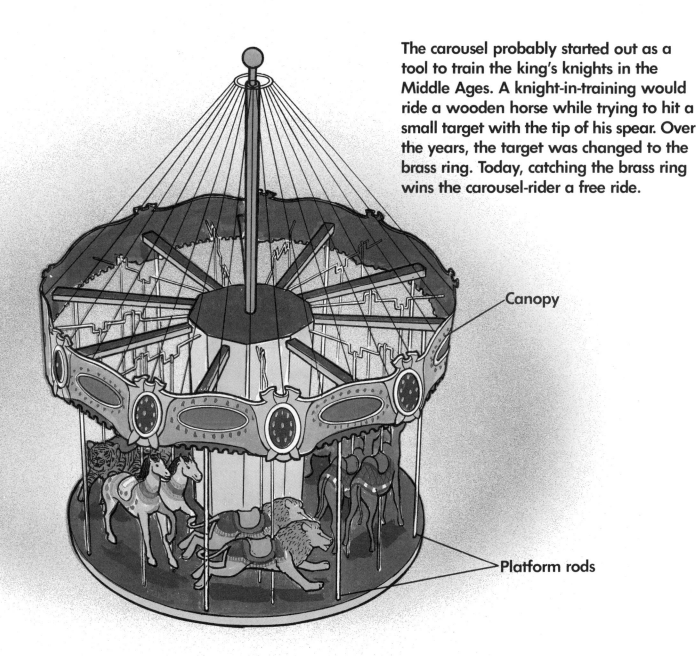

Canopy

Platform rods

Nearly all carousels (or merry-go-rounds) in use today run on electricity.

At the top and in the center of a carousel is a **shaft.** The shaft turns. A powerful electric motor turns the shaft. The motor starts and stops the ride and makes it go fast or slow.

A strong **ring** hangs from the top of the shaft. Steel **cables** connect the ring to the shaft. (A cable is a thick wire.)

A **platform,** round as a circle, hangs by steel **platform rods** from the ring overhead.

Under the **canopy** of the carousel, **cranks** stick out of the shaft. **Poles** are fixed to each crank, and animals are attached to the

poles. More than one pole can be attached to a crank. Each pole is attached to its own **arm** on the crank. The crank arm is a U-shaped part of the crank.

Each crank has a **gear** on the end. (A gear is a wheel with teeth.) The gears meet in the center of the carousel. The teeth of the gears from the cranks fit with the teeth of the shaft's **center gear.** As the center gear turns around, it turns the gears that are on the ends of the cranks.

The motor turns the platform and the gears turn the cranks. Because each animal is attached to its own crank arm, it goes up and down as the crank turns.

139

Movie projector

How does a movie projector show a film?

Movies were first called moving pictures, and that is what they still are today. A group of still photographs makes up a movie. Each picture is a little different from the pictures before and after it. As the pictures pass quickly before the eyes—24 pictures per second—the eyes and brain are fooled into seeing motion.

A movie projector shines a **light** through a moving strip of film to *project*, or show, the image onto a screen. Small holes run along one or both sides of the film strip. These holes match up with pins on a **sprocket wheel.** The sprocket wheel pulls the film through the projector.

The film is divided into frames. Each frame is a separate picture. The frames pass by the **gate.** The gate is the opening through which light shines out of the projector and onto the screen. The **shutter** uncovers the gate as each frame is pulled in front of it. The **lens** *focuses*, or makes clear, the picture. The shutter closes as the **divider** moves past the gate. The divider separates one frame from another. Each frame is in place as the gate opens. We see a moving picture.

A **projection reel** holds the film before it goes through the projector. After passing though the projector the film is wound onto a **take-up reel.** A full-length feature film may be stored on more than one reel.

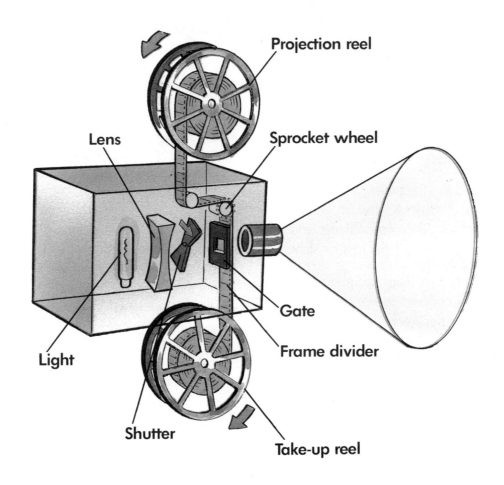

Projection reel

Lens

Sprocket wheel

Light

Gate

Frame divider

Shutter

Take-up reel

Elevator

How does an elevator go up and down?

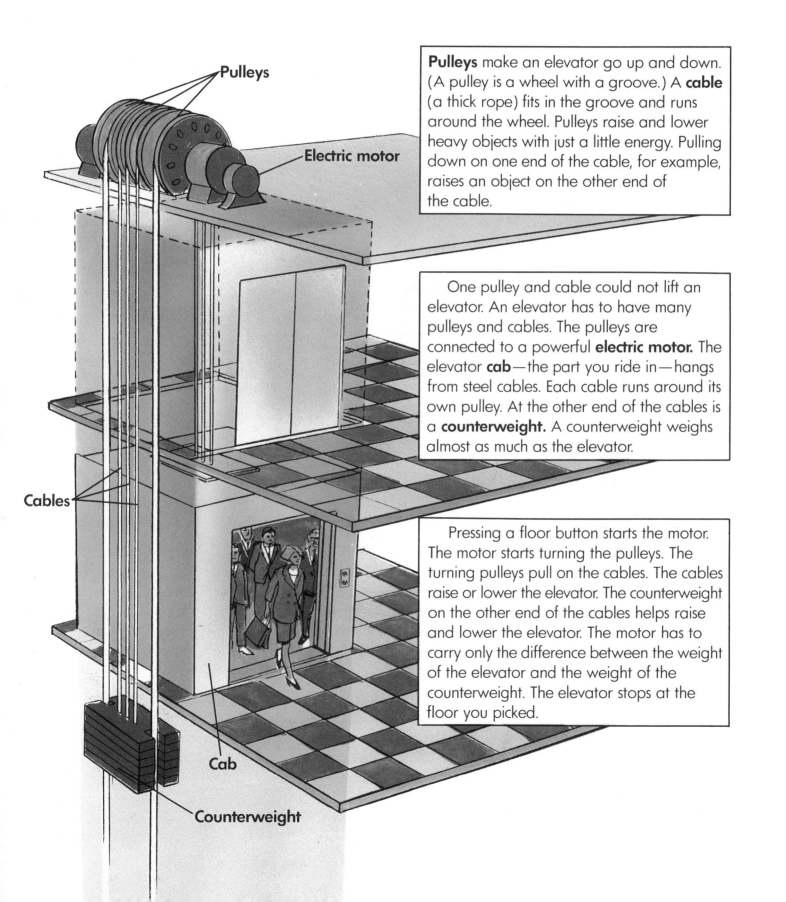

Pulleys

Electric motor

Cables

Cab

Counterweight

Pulleys make an elevator go up and down. (A pulley is a wheel with a groove.) A **cable** (a thick rope) fits in the groove and runs around the wheel. Pulleys raise and lower heavy objects with just a little energy. Pulling down on one end of the cable, for example, raises an object on the other end of the cable.

One pulley and cable could not lift an elevator. An elevator has to have many pulleys and cables. The pulleys are connected to a powerful **electric motor.** The elevator **cab**—the part you ride in—hangs from steel cables. Each cable runs around its own pulley. At the other end of the cables is a **counterweight.** A counterweight weighs almost as much as the elevator.

Pressing a floor button starts the motor. The motor starts turning the pulleys. The turning pulleys pull on the cables. The cables raise or lower the elevator. The counterweight on the other end of the cables helps raise and lower the elevator. The motor has to carry only the difference between the weight of the elevator and the weight of the counterweight. The elevator stops at the floor you picked.

Solar energy

How can solar energy heat homes, make electricity, and power cars?

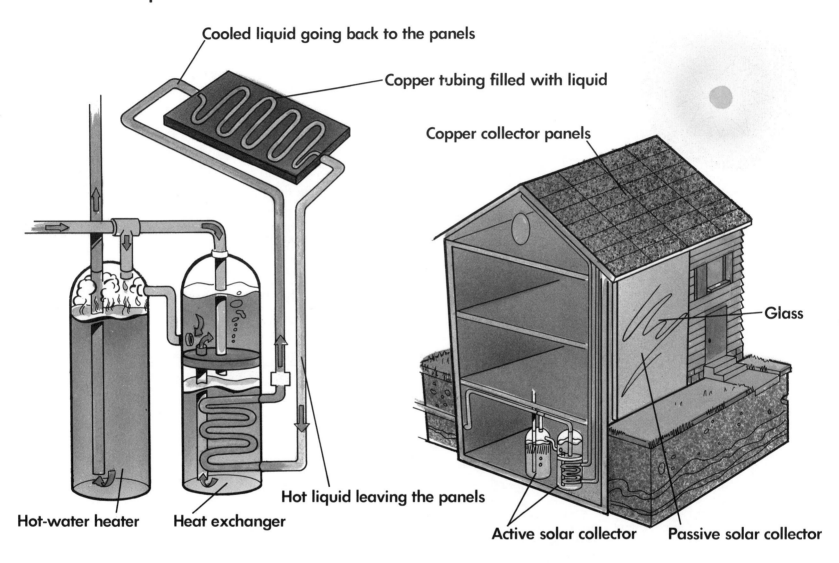

Cooled liquid going back to the panels

Copper tubing filled with liquid

Copper collector panels

Glass

Hot liquid leaving the panels

Hot-water heater

Heat exchanger

Active solar collector

Passive solar collector

The sun gives off energy. It is solar energy. The energy is in the form of sunlight. This energy can be collected and used. It can heat homes, make electricity, and even power cars! Sunlight can be collected all year around.

Using solar energy means using the sun's rays. The sun's rays can be collected with a **passive solar collector.** This kind of collector is used to heat homes. It is called "passive"

because it has no moving parts. It is made of a special **glass.** Sunlight comes in on one side, passes through, and heats the room on the other side. Very little heat leaves through the glass when the sun is not shining.

An **active solar collector** uses moving parts to collect the sun's energy. The moving parts are motors, fans, and pumps. This kind of collector is used to heat water for washing and bathing. **Copper collector panels** are placed on the roof of the house. **Copper tubes** filled with liquid run through the collectors. As the liquid travels through the tubing, it gets hot. The **hot liquid** goes to a **heat exchanger** (iks-CHAYN-jur). The heat exchanger warms a tank of water. The warmed water is pumped into a **hot-water heater.** It is stored there. The water may now be heated even more. The **cooled liquid** is pumped back to the collector panels for reheating. (The liquid does not freeze while running through the panels in the winter.)

Another type of solar collector changes sunlight into electricity. Cars that run on solar energy use these solar collector panels to collect energy. A motor runs the car. The motor is battery-powered. The battery gets its energy from the collector panels on the car. The battery stores the energy. The car runs on its stored energy even when the sun is not shining.

Imagine that gasoline—not water—flows over Niagara Falls. Imagine that the gas flows as fast as the water does—about five billion gallons an hour. Imagine that all this gas is collected and saved for 200 million years. If all that gas were then burned, the energy that it would give off would equal the energy the sun gives off in only one hour.

Collector panels

Cartoons

How are cartoons made?

Do you know your eyes "remember" things? It is true. For a split second, they hold onto the last image they saw. It is eye/brain memory that makes movies—and cartoons—work.

If a picture quickly takes the place of another picture, one after the other, the brain thinks it is seeing just one picture. If there are slight changes in each picture, the brain thinks it is seeing a moving picture. If the pictures (called "frames") are shown as fast as 24 frames per second, the image moves smoothly. If the pictures are shown slower than 24 frames per second, the image does not move smoothly.

A cartoon is frame after frame of drawings. An artist creates the drawings by hand, with pencils, inks, and paints. Some of today's computers can create the drawings as well. No matter how the frames are created, the cartoon is still a group of changing frames.

Drawing the frames takes a lot of time. Remember: The artist would have to draw 24 pictures for every second of film. A 90-minute film would have 129,600 drawings! It would take an artist drawing one frame every ten minutes—and that is fast—more than 11 years to draw the cartoon.

One way to cut down on the time it takes to create a cartoon is to paint on cels. Cels are clear plastic sheets. Only the changes between one frame of the cartoon and the next are painted on the cels. One (or a few) backgrounds are painted because the background changes less often. A cel is then placed over the background. The same thing is done with the next cel—which is a little

different—and the next cel after that, and so on. A movie camera makes a photograph of each cel against the background. The photographs then become the frames that make up the moving cartoon. You have seen that when Fred Flintstone drives through Bedrock, he drives past the same trees, rocks, and buildings over and over!

Another trick to save time is to keep each drawing simple. Drawing Mickey Mouse with four fingers is faster than drawing him with five.

With the invention of computers came the fastest and easiest way to make cartoons. A computer can store, or keep, information about how a character (KAYR-ik-tur) walks, runs, or flies. The computer then can draw the characters. The computer draws the character—in single frames—walking, running, or flying.

A script is written before a cartoon can be drawn. The script describes every scene and gives the words to the story. People read aloud from the script and are the voices of the characters. Many times, one person is the voice for many characters. As the people read the script, the sound is recorded. The cartoonist can then draw the faces of the characters to match the words being said. The mouth of the character changes as the reader's mouth changes.

Wind instruments

How do wind instruments make music?

Wind instruments use air pressure to make musical sounds. Most wind instruments are tubes through which air is blown. The air inside the tube is made to *vibrate*—to move back and forth.

Different vibrations make different sounds. A high-speed vibration makes a high note. A low-speed vibration makes a low note. These high and low speeds are *pitches* of notes (sounds). The length of the air column inside an instrument changes its pitch. The levers, holes, and slides on wind instruments change the distance air travels before leaving the tube. Some instruments are very short. They will never sound deep and low. And some are long. They will never blow a high note.

The wind instruments shown here are the **flute,** the **saxophone,** the **clarinet,** and the **trombone.**

A **trombone** is a brass instrument. A brass instrument has a cup-shaped mouthpiece. The musician blows through the mouthpiece. The lips must be held just right to make the air inside the tube vibrate. A trombone player moves a slide in and out to change the length of the tube. With the slide out, the air travels farther before it leaves. The note is low. With the slide pulled in, the note is high.

A musician playing a brass instrument also can change the pitch by changing lip position and by blowing harder or softer. This takes a lot of practice.

Oboes and **clarinets** are woodwind instruments. Covering the holes on its side changes the length of the air column of a woodwind. On an oboe and clarinet, pressing levers and keys covers the holes. The more holes that are covered, the farther

Flute

Trombone

Clarinet

Saxophone

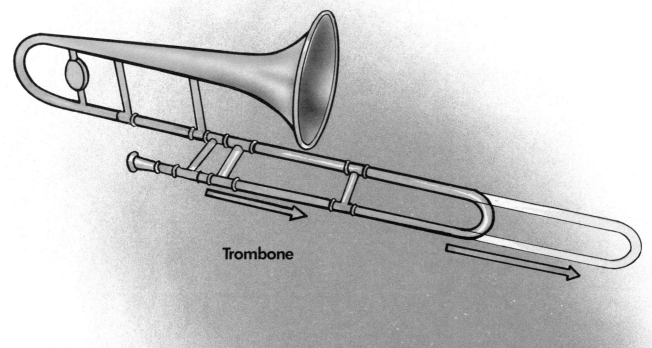

Trombone

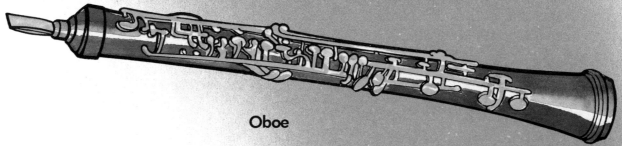

Oboe

the air must go to escape. The farther the air goes, the lower the note. When only the hole nearest the lips is open, the note is high. The lowest note is played with all the holes covered.

Some woodwinds have reeds fixed to their mouthpieces. A reed is a thin piece of cane or wood that vibrates when air is blown over it. Oboes and clarinets are reed instruments. The double reed of the oboe is its mouthpiece. A clarinet has one reed. The vibrating reed creates the air vibration that makes the tone in a wind instrument.

A **flute** has just a hole across which the musician blows air. Blowing air across this hole at the right angle starts the air vibrating inside the flute. The notes are made higher and lower by covering and opening the holes with keys and levers.

Flute

147

Videocassette recorder

How does a videocassette recorder record a TV show?

The tapes that go into a videocassette recorder (VCR) are plastic strips coated with rust particles. A VCR records the picture (video) part on tracks (paths). The video tracks run diagonally across the tape. The VCR records the sound (audio) part on a straight track. The electromagnets that record and play back the tape are called heads. (An electromagnet is a core, or center, of metal with wire wrapped around it. When electricity flows through the wire, the core turns into a magnet.)

The VCR is connected by **cables** (thick wire) to the antenna and to the TV set. Pushing the **videocassette** into the VCR flips a plastic flap up. The machine's arms pull the tape and wrap it around the recording/playback head. The tuner picks up the TV signals to be recorded from the **antenna.** The recording head arranges the particles of rust into a pattern that matches the signals for the picture. Another head records the sound signals. The rust patterns will then produce the picture signals through the playback head. The tuner then changes the VCR signals into TV signals. The signals are sent to the TV set.

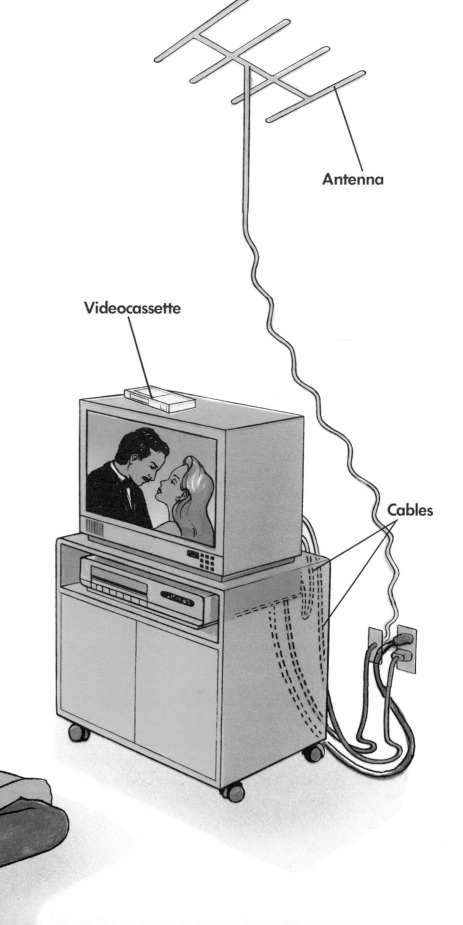

Antenna

Videocassette

Cables

148

Space suit

How does a space suit protect an astronaut out in space?

Out in space there is not enough air or heat for a human to live. A space suit surrounds an astronaut with an *atmosphere* (AT-muh-sfeer) in which he or she can live. (Atmosphere is the air that surrounds the Earth.) Each suit is made to fit the astronaut who will wear it.

The suit is made in several parts. The inner layer is the **liquid cooling and ventilation** (vent-uhl-AY-shuhn) **garment** (LCVG). A pump keeps the cooling liquid flowing through the LCVG. The LCVG keeps the astronaut at a comfortable, healthy temperature.

The outer shell of the suit is airtight. (Air cannot leak out of it.) It holds the air needed to keep the astronaut alive. Bottles attached to the back of the suit feed oxygen gas into the suit.

The outer shell is made in parts. The top part of the body has gloves. The pants have built-in boots. A **helmet** covers the astronaut's head. A microphone and earphones are built into the helmet. These let the astronaut talk with the shuttle crew. To operate the radio, the astronaut uses **controls** that are placed on the chest of the suit.

To move around in space—it has no gravity—an astronaut uses a **manned maneuvering** (muh-NOO-vur-ing) **unit** (MMU). (Without gravity, people float.) It is like a rocket-pack fastened onto the back of the suit. It moves the astronaut through space.

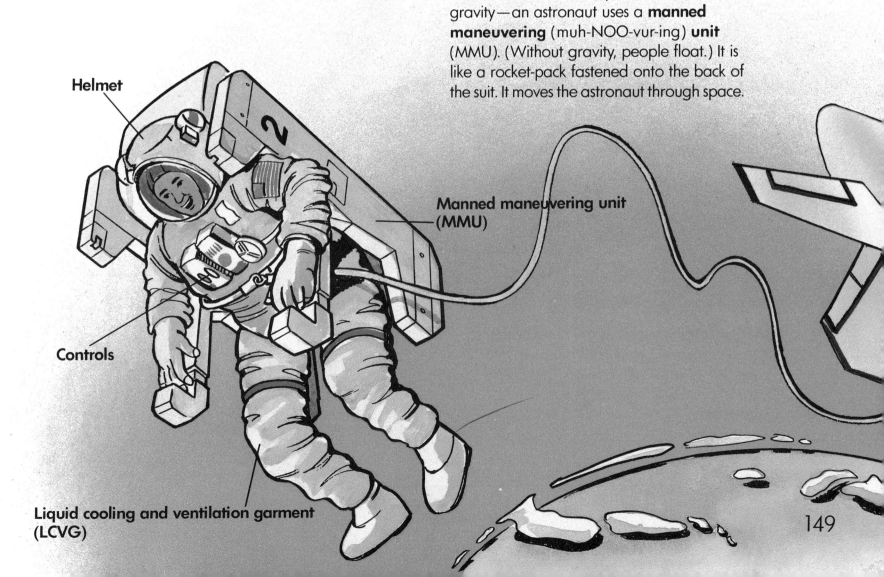

Helmet

Controls

Manned maneuvering unit (MMU)

Liquid cooling and ventilation garment (LCVG)

Pencil sharpeners

How do pencil sharpeners sharpen?

1. A **motor** runs an electric pencil sharpener.

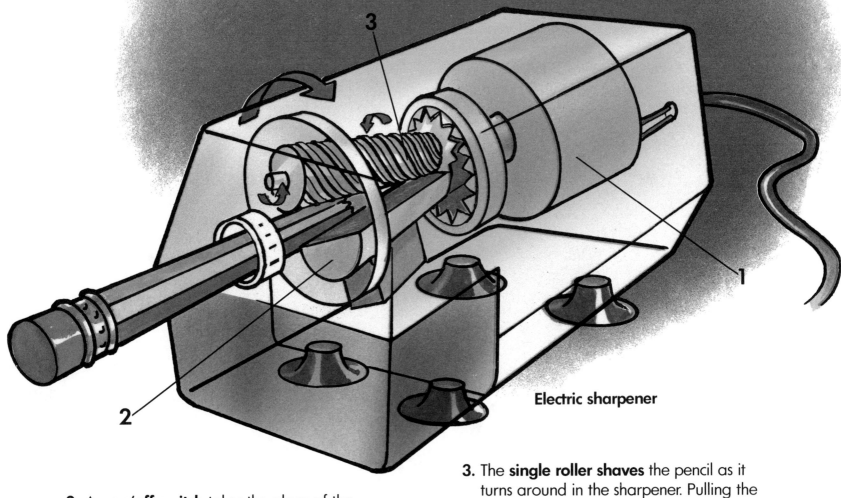

Electric sharpener

2. An **on/off switch** takes the place of the second roller. As the pencil is pushed into the hole, it presses the switch. The switch starts the motor, and the sharpener goes on.

3. The **single roller shaves** the pencil as it turns around in the sharpener. Pulling the pencil out stops the motor.

1. A pencil sharpener with a crank uses a pair of **rollers** to sharpen. The rollers have raised, sharp ridges.

2. The crank is connected to a **gear.** (A gear is a wheel with teeth.) This gear drives two smaller **gears**—one at the end of each roller.

3. As the **crank is turned,** the gears make the rollers turn. As the rollers turn, they carve the pencil between them.

4. There is enough space below the rollers for the pencil **shavings** to fall. The shavings fall to the bottom of the sharpener's cover.

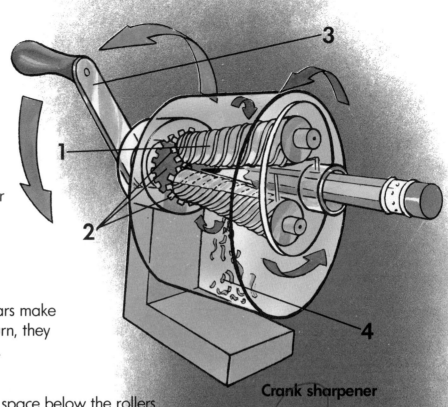

Crank sharpener

1. The simplest pencil sharpener—the one you hold in your hand—uses a **blade** to sharpen. The blade sits at an angle.

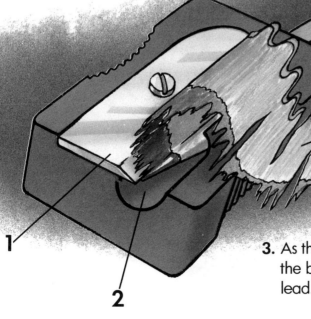

2. A **pointed hole** holds the pencil at just the right angle for sharpening.

3. As the **pencil is twisted** in the plastic box, the blade shaves off layers of wood and lead. The **shavings** curl out of the slot.

Hand-held sharpener

151

Light show

What are all the different lights in a light show?

The basic tools for stage lighting are the floodlight and the spotlight. "Floods" have wide beams that spread over a large area. "Spots" have narrow beams that light up just one person or object. Floods and spots both give off white light. For them to give off colors, gels are used. Gels are pieces of clear, colored plastic that are placed over the lamps.

At a concert, the lights are controlled by a computer. The computer is connected to the music's sound system. The lights can be made to flash and change in time with the music. A fog machine can be used, too.

A light beam passing through the fog looks almost solid. Many colored spots dancing in the fog can look magical!

Strobe lights add steady flashing to the light show. A strobe effect looks like a camera flash popping over and over. In the flashing of a strobe light, movement appears to slow down. Lasers are very narrow, strong, bright beams of light. The length of the beam can be seen even without a fog machine, since the beam bounces off even the tiniest particles in the air. Swirling through the air and fog, lasers can look like light sculptures!

Bar code scanner

How does a scanner read a bar code?

Each product in the store has a number. It is on the product's package. The number is a Universal Product Code (UPC). The UPC is made up of black stripes (bars) and white spaces. The store's computer reads these bar codes as numbers.

There are two kinds of scanners that read bar codes. Both kinds enter the name and price of the product into the cash register *automatically* (aht-uh-MAT-i-klee)—on their own. One kind of scanner looks like a space gun. The clerk aims the scanner at the code.

The other kind of scanner is built into the counter. The checker runs the bar code over a **glass plate** in the counter. The scanner sits under this glass plate. The scanner shines light from a **laser** onto **mirrors.** (A laser is a narrow, powerful light beam.) The mirrors reflect the light up through the glass plate and onto the bar code.

The white spaces between the black bars act like mirrors. They reflect the laser light

back into the scanner. The bars don't reflect the light. The scanner picks up the reflections from the white spaces. The computer "reads" the bars and the white spaces.

To help the scanner read the bar code, the laser beam shines through a **spinning disk.** (A disk is a round and thin plate.) It makes the bar code look *three-dimensional* (duh-MENCH-uh-nuhl), or lifelike, to the scanner. The product does not have to be held straight over the glass plate. The scanner can read the code at many angles.

The computer then changes the bar pattern into the code number for that product. Once the computer has the product's number, it looks up its name and price. They have already been listed in the store's computer. The computer finds the name and price and prints them out in less than a second! The scanner beeps when the computer has picked up the code. It is then ready to read the next bar code.

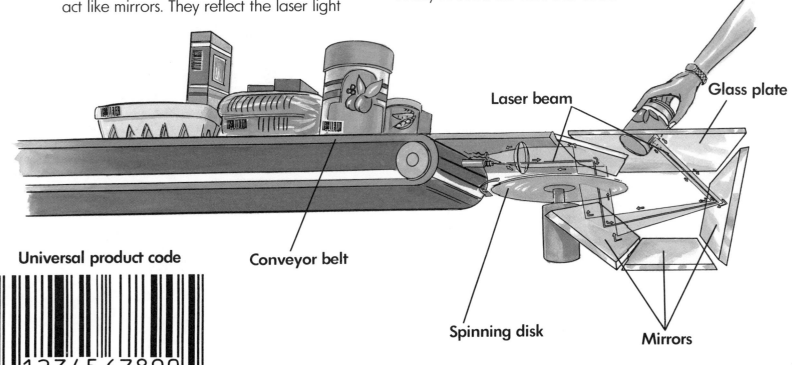

Laser beam

Glass plate

Universal product code

Conveyor belt

Spinning disk

Mirrors

1234567890

Special effects

How do movies create their special effects?

Some special effects are simple to do. Running film backward *reverses* the action. A swimmer jumps *out* of a pool and lands on her feet. Stopping the film and *replacing* a dog with a horse will look like the dog has *turned into* a horse when the film is shown.

For more complicated effects, many tricks are used together. To create a giant gorilla climbing up a building, a smaller model of the scene is used. A smaller model of the building is first built. It is placed in front of a background that looks real. A gorilla puppet is made to climb up the building. As the scene is *projected*, or shown, it doesn't look as though the building or gorilla is small.

See that giant lizard walking down the streets of the city? The first step in creating this special effect is to pick a background. People running away—from nothing—are filmed against the city background. This film is then projected against a two-way mirror. (A two-way mirror looks like a regular mirror from one side. It *reflects* images. It can be looked through from the other side.) The two-way mirror sits at an angle. A special screen reflects the picture. The screen sends the picture back through the two-way mirror to a movie camera.

The lizard—either a real lizard or a model—is placed in front of the screen. The size of the lizard that shows up in the movie can be changed. Changing the size of the buildings in the projected background changes the size of the lizard. The part of the projected background that shines on the lizard does not show up in the film. It is not bright enough. The part that reaches

the screen shows up brightly. What the movie camera "sees" is a lizard moving against a background of real people and real buildings.

Cut-out *mattes* (mats) in the shape of buildings or cars can be placed in front of the lizard. These mattes leave blank spaces on the film. Projected pictures of buildings or cars are added later. It looks as if the lizard is coming out from behind real buildings and cars. The final film image looks real!

Glossary

AILERON (AY-luh-rahn)

A flap on the back edge of an airplane wing that can be moved to control the plane's position in the air.

AIRFOIL (AYR-foyl)

A curved object (such as an airplane wing) that is shaped to create lift as it moves through the air.

AIR PRESSURE

The force of the surrounding air that pushes against everything on Earth.

AMPLIFIER (AM-pluh-fyr)

The part of a system (such as in a walkie-talkie or a record player) that increases the power of the sound signal before it is played back.

AMPLIFY

To make greater, stronger, or larger.

ANTENNA

The part of an electrical circuit (often a metal rod or coil) that picks up radio or television waves. The waves produce a small signal in the antenna.

ATMOSPHERE (AT-muh-sfeer)

The air that surrounds the Earth.

ATOM

Particles that are so tiny they are invisible to the eye. Everything is made up of atoms. Atoms are made up of electrons, protons, and neutrons. The protons and neutrons make up the center of the atom; the electrons circle around the center.

AUDIO (AHD-ee-o)

The sound part of a television program.

AUTOMATIC (aht-uh-MAT-ik)

Able to work on its own.

AXLE

The rod on which a wheel or pair of wheels turns.

BEAM

A stream of particles or waves, often made up of many rays (such as light rays).

BINARY SYSTEM

A counting system that uses only the numbers 0 and 1 to express all the numbers.

BUOYANCY (BOY-uhn-see)

The ability of an object to float to the top when placed underwater.

CABLE

A thick wire or rope.

CALIPER

A device made up of two plates that press against the sides of a turning wheel in some brake systems. Covering the inside of the plates is a material that is frictional—it causes the disk to slow down.

CEL

Clear plastic sheets on which only the changes between one frame of a cartoon and the next are painted.

CELL

A device in which electrical energy is stored, or held, in chemical form (such as a battery).

CIRCUIT (SUR-kuht)

A "loop" through which electricity flows.

COIL

Twisted wire, often in the shape of a spiral, that is used in electromagnets.

COMBUSTION (kuhm-BUHS-chuhn)

The process of burning to make heat and light.

COMPRESSION (kuhm-PRESH-uhn)

Forcing a large amount of gas or liquid into a much smaller space. This puts the gas or liquid at a much higher pressure, and energy is stored so it can be released.

CONCAVE

Having a surface that curves in.

CONDUCTOR

A substance that transmits, or sends from one place to another, some form of energy (such as electricity).

CONVECTION (kuhn-VEK-shuhn)

The spread of heat by the movement of gas molecules. When a gas is heated, the molecules move much faster. They take up a larger space. Because they spread out to take up a larger space, the gas is lighter. The hot gas rises and cooler gas takes its place, so the heat has "spread."

CONVERGING LENS

(kuhn-VURJ-ing LENZ)

A lens whose surface curves out, bending light rays so that they seem to come together at a farther point than they actually do.

CONVEX

Having a surface that curves out.

CORNEA (KOR-nee-uh)

The clear outer part of the eye that covers the iris (the colored part) and the pupil (the black center). It lets light into the inside of the eye.

COUNTERWEIGHT

A weight in a machine that is attached to a moving part to balance the weight of the moving part.

DECIMAL SYSTEM

(DES-uh-muhl SIS-tuhm)

A numbering system that is based on the use of ten numbers.

DEFLATE (dee-FLAYT)

To let the air out of; to flatten.

DEMODULATE (dee-MAHJ-oo-layt)

To separate the sound or radio signal from the carrier signal. To change the modulated signal into the original radio signal.

DIMENSION (duh-MEN-chuhn)

A measure of a distance in one direction. Humans see in three dimensions: height, width, and depth.

DISK

A thin, flat, round object.

ELECTRIC CHARGE

An amount of electricity. Adding electrons makes a negative charge; subtracting electrons makes a positive charge.

ELECTRIC CURRENT

The flow of electrons through a conductor such as wire.

ELECTRICITY

The movement of negatively charged particles called electrons toward positively charged particles called protons. Electricity is a form of energy.

ELECTRODE

A conductor through which electric current either flows into or out of an electrical device (such as a battery).

ELECTROLYTE (uh-LEK-tro-lyt)

A substance that conducts, or sends from one place to another, electricity.

ELECTROMAGNET

A core, or center, of metal with wire wound around it. Electricity running through the wire turns the core into a magnet.

ELECTRON

One of the three kinds of particles that make up an atom. An electron has a negative electric charge. Atoms have one or more electrons surrounding their center. The movement of electrons through a conductor such as a wire is electricity.

ELECTRON GUN

The device that sends a stream of electrons to the screen of a television.

ELECTRONIC EYE

A group of electrical devices that react to changes in light. The electronic eyes of some automatic doors open the door when someone steps in front of them and blocks the light.

ENERGY

The ability to do work.

ESCAPEMENT (uh-SKAYP-muhnt)

A wheel and anchor device in a clock or watch which controls and keeps constant the rate of motion of the gears.

EYEPIECE

The lens or set of lenses that is closest to the user's eye.

FOCAL LENGTH

The distance of a focus point from the lens.

FOCAL POINT

The point at which light rays come together after being bent and focused by a converging lens.

FOCUS

A position in which an object must be placed to be seen clearly.

FORCE

The push or pull that is placed on an object.

FREQUENCY (FREE-kwuhn-see)

The number of complete cycles per second—the speed—of a wave of sound.

FRICTION

The force between two objects that are touching each other.

FULCRUM

The part on which a lever turns or moves.

GAS

A substance (such as air) that has no shape and does not take up a space that can be measured. A gas either spreads throughout the air or flows out to the outline of its container.

GEAR

A wheel with teeth. It moves the power from the motor of a machine to the moving parts of the machine.

GENERATOR

A machine that changes mechanical energy into electrical energy. The wind that pushes a sailboat and the spring that unwinds to move the windup toy forward are examples of mechanical energy. Electricity is an example of electrical energy.

GRAVITY

The force that pulls us toward the Earth. Without gravity, we would float.

GYROSCOPIC FORCE

(jy-ro-SKAHP-ik FORS)
The force by which a spinning object spins in the same direction and at the same angle until gravity and friction slow it down.

HEAT EXCHANGER

(HEET iks-CHAYN-jur)
A set of pipes that allows a hot liquid or gas to warm a cool one or a cold liquid or gas to cool a hot one.

HYDROGEN

A gas that has no color or smell.

INCANDESCENCE (in-kuhn-DES-uhnts)

The giving off of light when the filament of a light bulb is heated.

INFLATE (in-FLAYT)

To fill with air; to blow up.

LASER

(Laser is an acronym—a word made from the first letters of the words it stands for—for Light Amplification by Stimulated Emission of Radiation.)
A narrow, powerful beam of light.

LENS

A device, usually made of see-through material such as glass or plastic, that collects and focuses light rays.

LEVER

A bar that rests on a point (a fulcrum). A lever is used to lift an object.

LIFT

The force acting on an airfoil that pushes up and against the pull of gravity.

MAGNETIC FIELD

The space around a magnet or a wire carrying electricity in which a magnetic force can be felt.

MAGNETISM (MAG-net-izm)

The ability of objects—usually metals—to pull toward or push away other objects.

MAGNETRON (MAG-nuh-trahn)

An electronic device that makes microwaves. The magnetron is one of the most important parts of a microwave oven.

MICROCHIP

A chip about the size of a fingertip upon which thousands of tiny electronic parts are connected to make up a circuit.

MICROPHONE

An instrument through which sound waves are made into an electric current to transmit (send) or record sound.

MICROPROCESSOR

(MY-kro-PRAH-ses-or)
The "brain" or central processing unit of a computer. It controls the flow of information and does arithmetic.

MICROWAVE

An electromagnetic wave with a wavelength shorter than those of radio waves. Microwaves are used to cook food.

Glossary

MODULATE (MAHJ-oo-layt)
To change a sound wave or radio signal so that it can be transmitted (sent) with a carrier signal.

MOLECULE (MAHL-i-kyool)
A particle that is so tiny it is invisible to the eye. Molecules are made of atoms that stick together. A molecule of water, for example, is made up of two hydrogen atoms and one oxygen atom.

NOZZLE
A short tube that speeds up or guides the flow of a liquid or gas.

OBJECTIVE LENS
The lens or set of lenses that is closest to the object being studied. It is the first lens or set of lenses to magnify the object.

OCULAR LENS (AHK-yu-lahr LENZ)
The lens or set of lenses that is in the eyepiece. It magnifies the image produced by the objective lens.

ORBIT
The regular path followed by an object traveling around Earth.

OXYGEN (AHK-si-juhn)
A colorless gas that makes up about 21 percent of the air we breathe.

PAWL
A machine part that works with a notch on a ratchet wheel to permit movement in only one direction.

PHOSPHOR (FAHS-fur)
A substance that gives off light when certain kinds of energy flow to it.

PHOTOCONDUCTOR
A substance that conducts, or sends from one place to another, electricity as light shines on it.

PITCH
How high or low a sound is.

POLARIZED LENS (PO-luh-ryzd LENZ)
A lens that lets through only the light whose waves are moving in a certain direction.

POLES, MAGNETIC
The two parts of a magnet where the magnetic force or field is the strongest.

PRISM (PRIZ-uhm)
A triangle of polished clear material (glass) that separates white light into the colors it is made up of: red, orange, yellow, green, blue, indigo, and violet.

PULLEY
A wheel with a grooved rim to hold a rope or chain. It changes the direction or the location of a pulling force.

RADIO WAVE
A wave with a wavelength longer than that of a microwave. Radio waves are used to transmit (send) signals.

RATCHET WHEEL
A toothed wheel that is held in place or turned by a pawl.

RECEIVE
To get or to accept.

RECEIVER
An electronic device that accepts incoming electromagnetic signals and changes then into a form that can be seen or heard.

RETINA (RET-i-nuh)
The "movie screen" of the eye. The back wall of the eye upon which an image focuses. It receives the image formed by the lens and is connected to the brain.

SATELLITE
An electronic device put into orbit around Earth to study parts of the Earth from outer space.

SIGNAL
An electric current that is changed to form a code for transmitting (sending) information.

SOLENOID (SO-luh-noyd)
An electromagnetic device—a coil (loop) of wires with a metal rod inside—that changes electrical energy into mechanical energy. Electricity is an example of electrical energy. The wind that blows a sailboat is an example of mechanical energy.

SOUND WAVES
Changes in pressure that travel through the air or other materials. When these "pressure waves" reach our ears, a matching vibration is made in our eardrums. The brain understands these vibrations to be sound.

SPROCKET
A toothed wheel that works with a chain to pull something open or closed, forward or backward, up or down. Also, a toothed wheel that fits in the holes of something (such as film) to move it through a machine (such as a projector).

THERMOSTAT (THUR-muh-stat)
A device that makes sure the temperature of a room, area, or instrument stays the same.

TRANSFORMER (tranz-FOR-mur)
A device that changes an electric current from one voltage to another voltage.

TRANSMIT
To send.

TRANSMITTER
An electronic device that changes a sound wave into an electrical signal that can be sent.

TURBINE (TUR-buhn)
An engine that, like a wheel, turns on an axis. The engine has a shaft with blades. The blades are moved by the pressure of a gas or liquid (such as air or water). As the blades turn, the shaft turns.

VIBRATE (VY-brayt)
To move back and forth or from side to side.

VIDEO (VID-ee-o)
The picture part of a television program.

VOLTAGE
The pressure or force that bumps electricity through a conductor.

X RAY
An electromagnetic wave with a wavelength that is very short. X rays are used to take pictures of the inside of a person's body.

Index